The Grieving Teen

A GUIDE FOR TEENAGERS
AND THEIR FRIENDS

Helen Fitzgerald

A Fireside Book
Published by Simon & Schuster
New York   London   Toronto   Sydney   Singapore

FIRESIDE
Rockefeller Center
1230 Avenue of the Americas
New York, NY 10020

FIRESIDE and colophon are registered trademarks of Simon & Schuster, Inc.

Designed by William Ruoto

Manufactured in the United States of America

3 5 7 9 10 8 6 4 2

Library of Congress Cataloging-in-Publication Data
Fitzgerald, Helen.
The grieving teen : a guide for teenagers and their friends / Helen Fitzgerald.
p. cm.
"A Fireside book."
Includes bibliographical references and index.
1. Grief in adolescence—Juvenile literature. 2. Bereavement in adolescence—
Juvenile literature. 3. Loss (Psychology) in adolescence—Juvenile literature.
4. Teenagers and death—Juvenile literature. [1. Grief. 2. Death.
3. Loss. (Psychology)] I. Title.

BF724.3.G73 F58 2000
155.9'37'0835—dc21   00-038746

ISBN 0-684-86804-0

Acknowledgments

Teenagers have been the source of the inspiration and much of the material that went into this book. Their personal accounts of the sad events that sent them into grief have touched me, as I'm sure they will you, and the steps they have taken toward recovery might blaze a trail for you to follow in your struggle toward a new life.

Among the teens and young adults who have helped me in preparation of this book were Eleanor Abrams, Karen Beardsley, Yael Flusberg, Samantha Gavin, Angela Glascock, and Denise Hershman, as well as many others I have met with privately or worked with in the teen groups that I conduct for the Mount Vernon Center for Community Mental Health in Fairfax County, Virginia. Necessarily, the identities of those whose experiences are related here have been altered to protect everyone's privacy.

I am also indebted to many others who have helped me get the time and the freedom from distraction to write the book. In particular, I am grateful to my friends Lee and Elaine Wick for providing my husband and me with the use of their wonderful mountain home in New Hampshire to get it started, and to John and Carol Pflug for the use of their beautiful condominium at Key Biscayne, Florida, as the project was moving along. In both cases, their generosity freed me for some crucial weeks from a constantly ringing telephone and the pressures that go with administering a grief program for a population of 950,000 people, including about 130,000 teenagers.

My editor at Simon & Schuster, Caroline Sutton, was very supportive of this project, as was my agent, Anne Edelstein, and I am grateful to both of them for encouraging me to proceed with it.

Finally, there is my husband, Richard Olson, who, as always, played a big part in convincing me to write the book and helped me with editorial suggestions and advice throughout.

This book is dedicated to all of the volunteers over more than two decades who have made it possible for me to minister to the needs of grieving people.

Contents

FOREWORD BY EARL A. GROLLMAN   15

INTRODUCTION   17

CHAPTER 1: WHEN LIFE HANGS IN THE BALANCE   23

1.	NOT KNOWING IF YOU WANT TO KNOW	23
2.	REACTING TO THE NEWS	25
3.	SHOULD YOU TELL YOUR FRIENDS?	26
4.	SHOULD YOU TELL YOUR TEACHERS?	26
5.	ARE YOU THE REAL PARENT?	27
6.	YOUR SOCIAL LIFE	28
7.	WHO ELSE CAN YOU TALK TO?	29
8.	SUPPORT GROUPS	30
9.	THE HOSPICE MOVEMENT	31
10.	FEELING SCARED	31
11.	HOSPITAL VISITS	32
12.	THE $64,000 QUESTION: AM I GOING TO DIE?	33
13.	HELPING YOUR SIBLINGS	34
14.	FEELING ANGRY	35
15.	SAYING GOOD-BYE	35
16.	SHOWING THAT YOU CARE	37

CHAPTER 2: WHEN DEATH COMES — 39

17.	DISCOVERING THE BODY	39
18.	DO I WANT TO BE THERE WHEN HE DIES?	40
19.	WHAT HAPPENS NEXT?	41
20.	WHAT IS DEATH LIKE FOR THE DYING PERSON?	42
21.	WHAT DOES A DEAD BODY LOOK OR FEEL LIKE?	43
22.	WHY AM I SO WEAK AND JITTERY?	44
23.	WHEN DEATH IS SUDDEN	44
24.	HOW YOU FOUND OUT	45
25.	I CAN'T BELIEVE THAT THIS HAS HAPPENED	47
26.	NO TIME TO SAY GOOD-BYE	47
27.	DO YOU WANT TO KNOW THE DETAILS?	49
28.	FLASHBACKS OR NIGHTMARES	50
29.	WHEN YOU CAN'T CRY	51

CHAPTER 3: FUNERALS, FORMALITIES, AND FAREWELLS — 55

30.	WHY DO WE HAVE FUNERALS?	55
31.	BUT WHAT IF IT HURTS TOO MUCH?	56
32.	HELPING YOURSELF BY GETTING INVOLVED	57
33.	THE VIEWING, VISITATION, OR WAKE	59
34.	SITTING SHIVA	61
35.	MEMORIAL SERVICES	62
36.	THE BURIAL SERVICE	63
37.	VISITING THE GRAVE	66
38.	CREMATION	67
39.	THE HEADSTONE	68

CHAPTER 4: UNDERSTANDING YOUR GRIEF **71**

40. WHAT IS GRIEF? WHAT IS MOURNING? 71
41. HOW LONG IS GRIEF? 72
42. AM I NORMAL? 74
43. WHO AM I? I FEEL DIFFERENT 75
44. I CAN'T SLEEP 77
45. WHAT ABOUT DREAMS? 78
46. I CAN'T EAT 78
47. I CAN'T REMEMBER ANYTHING 80
48. I CAN'T CONCENTRATE 81
49. CLOSE CALLS WHILE DRIVING 82
50. RESPONSES TO EXPECTED VERSUS SUDDEN DEATH 83
51. YOUR RELATIONSHIP WILL AFFECT YOUR GRIEF 85

CHAPTER 5: UNDERSTANDING YOUR FEELINGS **89**

52. SHOCK AND DISBELIEF 89
53. DENIAL: I WON'T ACCEPT THIS 91
54. ANGER: LIFE STINKS; IT'S NOT FAIR 94
55. GUILT AND REGRETS 98
56. DEPRESSION: I AM TOO SAD TO MOVE 103
57. I WANT TO DIE, TOO 106
58. FEARS AND WORRIES: I HAVE SO MANY CONCERNS 109
59. PHYSICAL SYMPTOMS 111

CHAPTER 6: ON RESUMING YOUR LIFE **113**

60. HOW BEST TO ANNOUNCE THE NEWS 114
61. YOUR FIRST DAY BACK 115
62. YOUR GRADES 116

63. YOUR HOMEWORK   117
64. HELPING YOUR FRIENDS HELP YOU   119
65. WHAT HAPPENS WHEN YOU SEE A COUNSELOR?   121
66. MANAGING YOUR STRESS   123

CHAPTER 7: WHY DOES IT HAVE TO BE SO HARD?   129

67. POSTPONING GRIEF   129
68. REMINDERS OF YOUR LOSS   131
69. IS IT OK TO ASK FOR KEEPSAKES?   132
70. WHEN DEATH COMES AT A REALLY BAD TIME   133
71. WHEN MORE THAN ONE PERSON HAS DIED   135
72. WHEN YOU CAN'T ATTEND THE FUNERAL   136
73. DEALING WITH THE PRESS   138
74. THE DEATH OF SOMEONE FAMOUS   139
75. HOLIDAYS, BIRTHDAYS, AND ANNIVERSARIES   140
76. DREAMS AND NIGHTMARES   142
77. TRICKS OF THE MIND   145

CHAPTER 8: TIGHTENING THE SCREWS   147

78. IF YOU WITNESSED THE DEATH   147
79. SURVIVOR GUILT: I SHOULD HAVE DIED INSTEAD   149
80. I CAUSED THE DEATH   151
81. SECRETS DISCOVERED AFTER A DEATH   154
82. DEALING WITH SUICIDE   156
83. MY BROTHER DIED OF AIDS   160
84. DEALING WITH MURDER   161
85. WHAT IS POST-TRAUMATIC STRESS DISORDER (PTSD)?   164

CHAPTER 9: WHAT DOES THE FUTURE HOLD FOR ME? 169

86. WHAT IF MY PARENT STARTS DATING? 170
87. MAYBE SOME GUY WILL TAKE ADVANTAGE OF MY MOM 172
88. MOM IS GETTING MORE CALLS FOR DATES THAN I AM 172
89. I HAVE A CRUSH ON THE GUY WHO MOM IS DATING 173
90. I FEEL DISLOYAL TO MY MOM 173
91. MY DAD IS GETTING MARRIED 174
92. LIVING WITH A STEPPARENT 174
93. WILL I EVER BE HAPPY AGAIN? 175
94. HOW DO I KNOW THAT I AM GETTING BETTER? 175

CHAPTER 10: TEENS AND THEIR SECRETS 179

95. MEGAN 179
96. SCOTT 181
97. NATALIE 183
98. CYNTHIA 184
99. KAREN 187

CHAPTER 11: WHAT FRIENDS CAN DO 193

100. SHOULD YOU TALK ABOUT WHAT HAPPENED? 195
101. PRACTICAL HELP YOU CAN PROVIDE 195
102. WHAT DO YOU TELL OTHER PEOPLE? 196
103. RELAYING WORD TO THE SCHOOL 196
104. KEEP AN EYE ON HOW YOUR FRIEND IS COPING 197
105. WHAT CAN YOU DO IF IT WAS YOUR FRIEND WHO DIED? 197
106. SECRETS TOO BIG TO HANDLE 198
107. DON'T GET INTO A SORROW COMPETITION 198

108. ARE YOU WORRIED ABOUT SAYING
     SOMETHING STUPID?   199
109. OTHER THINGS TO AVOID   200
110. SOME GOOD THINGS TO SAY AND DO   201
111. BEING A FRIEND CARRIES RESPONSIBILITIES   203

CHAPTER 12: IS THAT ALL THERE IS?   **205**

RESOURCE LIST: HELPFUL BOOKS AND WEB SITES   209
OTHER BOOKS ON TEEN GRIEF   209
WEB SITES ON GRIEF   209
WEB SITES WITH INFORMATION ABOUT FUNERAL
  PRACTICES IN VARIOUS FAITHS   210
INDEX   213

Foreword

For most teens, one of the joys of the teenage years is the feeling of being connected to others—not just parents and family, but friends, classmates, schools, clubs, and teams. It's what makes this time of a person's life so special and why in later years adults reminisce so much about their own teen years. For many people, life never again provides the richness of friendships and the camaraderie that they enjoyed in those years between thirteen and nineteen.

A death in the family can change all that. The terminal illness of a sister or the divorce of one's parents can do the same. Suddenly, families have to move or responsibilities are shifted such that there is little time left to spend with friends. One's inner world can change overnight, dimming the prospect for college, perhaps, and robbing one of the carefree years that one once thought still lay ahead. Of course, the loss of a loved one can make all of this seem selfish and unimportant—but it's not: these issues need to be brought out into the open.

Also, there is another part of teenage grief that makes it different from that of, say, adults. When tragedy strikes a family, the parents usually get the most attention. Adult friends gather with support for the widow or widower. If a child has died, it is the parents, again, who usually get the most attention from friends and relatives. Teenagers who are themselves approaching adulthood are all too often left to deal with their own grief alone. And the grief that they have to endure may be made worse by the fact that others don't seem to see it.

In earlier books, Helen Fitzgerald has offered her wise counsel, based on years of individual and group counseling, to the parents of younger children and to adults mourning the loss of loved ones. It is the grieving teen, caught up in life-shattering grief, whom she addresses in this book, one of the first to take a comprehensive look at the special needs of teenagers. The anger, guilt, and regrets that they feel, the loneliness, shock, and disbelief are all here. And throughout, the author offers sound, creative ideas on what a teen can do to work through his or her grief.

I have followed the career of Ms. Fitzgerald for most of the twenty-two years since she pioneered the nation's first grief program in a community mental-health center. That program continues today as part of the Mental Health Services of Fairfax County, Virginia. As coordinator, Ms. Fitzgerald has counseled hundreds, perhaps thousands, of teenagers, both individually and in groups, and has helped their families, friends, and siblings support them in their grief. She knows just about every personal tragedy that could befall any young person, and she brings to her work a level of understanding and empathy that others only wish that they could emulate.

If you are a teen looking for help with your own grief, feeling resentful, angry, or guilty, wondering if you have a future, this book can help you come to understand your feelings, discharge your anger, and start a new life from the ashes of sorrow and loss.

Earl A. Grollman,
author of *Straight Talk About Death for Teenagers*
Belmont, Massachusetts
November 1999

Introduction

In an earlier book, I wrote about a fifteen-year-old named Laura, whose unhappy situation as a young person whose needs were ignored continues to haunt me, for stories like hers remain largely unaddressed in the many books that have been written about death and dying. What Laura's story represents is the young person set somehow adrift by the illness or death of a loved one—not intentionally, of course, but set adrift nonetheless. As Laura cried out in that story, "I'm hurting, too."

Today, it seems that there are more than a few Lauras out there, shattered and set adrift by the violence that has become almost commonplace in our country. I think of the friends and classmates, sisters and brothers whose lives were changed forever by crazed gunmen at places like Columbine High School in Colorado, Heath High School in Georgia, or Thurston High School in Oregon—places once distant but now strangely united in tragedy. And I think of all those who have lost relatives and friends through accidents, illness, and self-inflicted wounds. It is for you, the Lauras or Bills or Elizabeths—teenagers whose lives have been caught up in personal tragedy, who have been alienated even from grieving loved ones—that I have written this book.

Teenagers—I almost recoil at using the word because it seems to lump everyone between thirteen and nineteen into a single group—often find themselves in the same role as Laura. Somehow, at a time when these emerging adults are just learning who they are, the adults around them might be equally uncertain as to how to deal with them. The result can come across as indifference, and it can be very painful and isolating.

Also, sad to state, genuine conflicts arise in families, pitting siblings against one another, or parents against children. Not every feeling of alienation is based on misunderstanding: sometimes parents really *are* unfair; sometimes siblings really *intend* to make your life miserable.

Is this the way you're feeling? If it is, let me see if I can refine it a bit. Someone you love has died or is dying. It may be your father or mother, brother or sister, grandparent, close friend, boyfriend, or girlfriend. It is someone whose life was a part of your life, whose dreams and aspirations were, to some extent, your dreams and aspirations. And that person's death or expected death is having a devastating effect on you and your own pursuit of a meaningful life.

Let's go further. You are finding that your family seems to have no time for you, that your suffering is being ignored, that everything about your life seems bent out of shape, that you have had to abandon things that were important to you, that your very sense of identity has been shaken, and yet nobody—even your best friends—seems to care. Does any of that hit the mark?

Are you feeling ashamed because of your changed circumstance? Stigmatized? Excluded from things that you were once part of? Made to assume a new role or roles that you are not comfortable with?

Growing up is pretty much a full-time job. You start out as a child dependent on parents for everything. You end up as an adult, fully independent, capable of becoming a parent yourself. It's a big change, and it doesn't happen overnight. Legally, you may still be classified as a child, but as each day passes, you are that much more of a complete adult. Your thoughts and opinions are important, and so are your feelings. They won't suddenly become important the day you turn twenty or twenty-one; they're important now. If someone you love has died, or is dying, your thoughts and feelings are just as legitimate and just as important as those of any of the adults around you.

So what are you thinking at this moment? And how are you feeling?

Much as we would like to believe that the right upbringing, good behavior, diligence, careful planning, and hard work earn a person happiness, it doesn't work that way. Life can bring rude surprises, shocking and painful losses for which there is no adequate preparation. If this describes what has happened to you, I can only say that it's OK to be bitter, it's OK to be angry, and it's OK to wonder what the heck life is all about. I have been there.

When my first husband died, I had two teenage daughters and two younger children. Looking back, I realize that they felt far more deeply about their father's illness and death, and about the attention or lack of attention that they were getting, than I perceived in that trying time. I know that my teenage daughters had new roles—especially meal preparation and housecleaning—thrust on them when I entered the workplace for the first time to replace some of my dying husband's lost income. Even so, I was like a lot of parents today who somehow assume that their children—even the older ones—are incapable of handling bad news, limiting them to shorthand summaries yet expecting them to adjust to painful changes in their lives. And I was like all those parents who are so caught up in their own impossible webs of mounting concerns that they fail to feel or fully understand the terrible pain and confusion being experienced by their children. I wish now that I had had a better understanding of what was happening to my own and that, in addition, they would have had a book like this to turn to. That's why I have written this book. I would like to help you express your great sadness and loss and in time to find new meaning and direction for your life.

As a mother and grandmother, I don't pretend to know all there is to know about the life of a teenager today. I certainly don't know about your specific life. But I have helped many young people in the course of my work in a community grief program, and I vividly remember what it was like to be a teenager. It was a great time in my life, but it was also a time when I was filled with much uncertainty about the future, because my parents saw no need for me to go to college. If my future husband hadn't shown up at our farm to buy a dog, I might have married and remained in that town for the rest of my life. That would have been all right, but by venturing out into the world, I have had opportunities that I would not have had there, such as the work that I have been doing for the last twenty-two years: helping people like you. Fortunately, no one close to me died while I was growing up. My children were not so lucky. And you may not be so lucky either.

I have learned a lot about teenagers from teenagers. Sharing with me the confusion they are experiencing, the bitterness and resentment they sometimes feel toward their parents, the longing for a return to the way things were before illness or death struck, they have made me aware that losses inflicted on a person at this time of life can be particularly devastating. In spite of this, most of these same young people have been able to rebuild their lives over time, and their stories might help you do the same.

Like my other books, this one is organized to help you find the help you need when you need it. The table of contents, index, and cross-reference system will steer you to help on whatever is hurting the most. Later, you can return to the beginning and read it as you would any other book. I have found that this kind of organization has been very helpful to my readers, and I hope that this will be true for you as well.

The Grieving Teen

Chapter 1

WHEN LIFE HANGS IN THE BALANCE

For a young person especially, grief can come as a terrible shock. As you might have learned, it doesn't wait for formalities. It can hit you—*wham!*—with the first shocking news of an impending death. If someone you love is critically ill and possibly facing death, and you know it, you are almost certainly grieving right now. Or you might be in a kind of limbo where you aren't sure how to feel or what to believe. And if those around you seem to be unaware of how you are feeling, your world may be spinning right now.

If any of this is happening to you, it's an anxious time that you're going through. I don't necessarily have all of the answers, but here are some things that you can do to ease your anxiety and make the most of the time that you may have left with your loved one.

1. NOT KNOWING IF YOU WANT TO KNOW

Has someone in your family been ill for a very long time? Have you noticed that hospital visits have become more frequent and last longer? Have you noticed grim facial expressions and hushed telephone conversations and wondered what was going on? If so, join the club. This happens a lot, because people are in shock, uncertain about what to say and when to say it. It's understandable, but for a young family member left in the dark, it can be both confusing and hurtful.

It will help you to reflect on the dilemma that exists in the minds of parents and grown-up relatives when grim developments are occurring. Often a boy or girl will not want too much information because the implications are too frightening. But if you know only bits and pieces of what is happening, you might worry more than necessary, imagining things to be even worse than they are. For example, even if a loved one is going to die, it can be reassuring to know that the person is not in great pain or to know that you will have a chance to say good-bye. It can also be reassuring to know that you are not in any way responsible for what has happened.

On the other hand, parents sometimes give too much information, going into too much detail. This, too, can be upsetting. I know of a father whose son died many years ago, yet he still doesn't know how fast his son's friend was driving when their car went off the road or whether his son was wearing his seat belt; these things are irrelevant to him. What's relevant is that his son is dead. Drawing the line between too little and too much is never easy for the bearers of such bad news, and this is especially true when they are passing information to someone whose ability to handle it is unclear.

What You Can Do

If you are caught up in such a tug-of-war, here is a thought. First, try to understand the turmoil brewing in the minds of your parent or parents, other family members, or friends who might possess the troubling information that you only suspect. It could be that they feel that you are too young, too fragile, or too frightened to know the truth. Second, demonstrate your own maturity and strength by relieving them of that anxiety, approaching the forbidden subject yourself. Third, give them the reassurance they need to be open with you. If you feel that you can handle the truth, tell them so. If you feel that you can't handle it, tell them that, too.

2. REACTING TO THE NEWS

No one wants to hear bad news, and yet, sooner or later, we all will. When you are told that a loved one is likely to die, how are you going to react? Gasp? Scream? Throw a tantrum? Go off to your room and cry?

I remember that when I told my children that their father would probably die, one of my teenagers replied, "Can we get a kitten?" Her response surprised me because it seemed so uncaring and unlike this daughter, who ordinarily was so loving and considerate of others. Years later, I found the answer in an essay that she did for a college course: she wrote that she wanted to think of something pleasant rather than concentrate on this grim news and what it would mean for all of us. Since then, working with many young people like her, I have come across many examples of seemingly inappropriate responses like this. I say "seemingly" because, in fact, they may be perfectly normal responses for a person who needs time to adjust mentally and physically to life-shattering news.

What You Can Do

Don't be embarrassed or ashamed if you react in some such "inappropriate" way when you are told that a loved one might be dying. You might find it necessary to focus on something else for a while, to buy time for accepting what you see as unacceptable. If it is more than you can bear to think about right now, that's OK. Read a book. Take a walk. Surf the Internet. Play basketball. Go to the movies. Paint a picture. Write a poem. Call a friend. In time, you will be able to deal with the news, but until then, take care of yourself. When you have done that, you may be able to help your parent or parents, brothers, or sisters who will be suffering too. Helping others may give you the greatest relief of all.

3. SHOULD YOU TELL YOUR FRIENDS ?

To tell or not to tell! Knowledge that a loved one is dying is a huge burden to carry by yourself. No matter how you may be feeling, it is not a disgrace to have an ailing parent; it is not a disgrace to have someone in your family die. Friends who know what you are going through will be far better able to give you caring and understanding support. On the other hand, if you don't tell them, they might be hurt and even angry that you didn't trust them enough to share this news with them. They might also sense your sadness, but misinterpret it as something else, perhaps as a sign that something is wrong with your relationship.

What You Can Do

While it isn't necessary to tell the whole world that someone you care about is dying, it is a good idea to share this news with those friends who are closest to you. To be sure, their responses will vary. Some will know instinctively what to do, but others will not know what to do or say. In such a case, you can help them and yourself by suggesting what they might do to help. Also, gently let them know what is not helpful. Remember, your friends wouldn't be your friends if they didn't care about you. Give them a chance to prove that they care, even if in this new and strange situation they might say something that comes across as harsh or even inconsiderate.

4. SHOULD YOU TELL YOUR TEACHERS?

Unless they know what is going on, your teachers cannot provide you with the support you need during a time of family crisis. If your grades slip, they may conclude that you have become an indifferent student or otherwise misinterpret what is going on. They won't know how to help you get through a difficult time in your life.

What You Can Do

Have private conferences with your teachers and counselors to tell them what is happening. Teachers are willing to work with you to help you keep up with schoolwork. It's important that you not fall seriously behind, and they can help you avoid doing so. Their understanding and support can make a big difference.

5. ARE YOU THE REAL PARENT?

Roles and duties often change when a family member becomes seriously ill. You might feel right now that you are the parent and your parents are your children. You might be the one who is attending to the needs of younger brothers and sisters. This can be confusing, as it was for my fourteen-year-old daughter when her father got sick. When I was away at work, I needed her to keep an eye on her younger brother and sister. But when I was home and she attempted to do the same thing, I would take over. All of this was frustrating to her and confusing to her younger siblings.

If there is someone in your family who is terminally ill, you might be expected to take on more jobs around the house than you had before—mowing the lawn, doing the laundry, or even taking over the grocery shopping. This could affect your studies or your after-school activities or deprive you of time to be with your friends. You may well resent the changes that are taking place in your life.

What You Can Do

You might have a talk with your parent or parents to discuss how best to prioritize the jobs needing attention and how to accomplish them with the least disruption to each person's normal activities. Or suggest a family meeting. If there is agreement on this, come prepared with a list of things that need to be done and ideas on how all of you, working together, can manage the tasks at hand. Family meetings can serve a valuable role, too, in sharing information and offering praise and encouragement for deserving efforts. You can help the cause by steering the meeting away from the sniping and complaining that often take place among siblings. For example, you can agree on some ground rules at the outset: only constructive things to be said about one another and no personal attacks.

If you now have the job of planning and cooking the meals, get familiar with the grocery store and check out the convenience foods that can be cooked quickly in the microwave (if you have one). With the approval of your parent or parents, even laundry can be done by younger children once they have been taught a routine. It would be worth the effort to do so, and, at the same time, performing this important function will give them a feeling of being part of the total family effort. This kind of planning takes time, of course, but it will save even more of your and others' time later.

6. YOUR SOCIAL LIFE

When someone is seriously ill or dying at your house, you may no longer have the freedom to invite your friends to visit. In fact, you might never be sure from day to day how your ill family member will be feeling or acting. It is frustrating to have to make so many changes. My late husband suffered from a brain tumor that affected his personality, making his temperament unpredictable. We never knew from minute to minute whether he was going to be in a good or bad mood. In a situation such as this, friends may prefer not to be around—and you might not want them to be.

What You Can Do

- Life can really be a merry-go-round in times like this. If you find it uncomfortable or even impossible to invite friends into your home, it might be possible for you to spend more time at their homes instead. Discuss this with your parent or parents, and work out a plan, as this will allow you to see your friends and save you from feeling guilty for not being home more.
- Spending time with your friends on the phone is another way to deal with this problem. Work out a plan with your parent or parents to make sure that the phone is available to them when they need it for important calls. If you don't have call waiting, your parents might want to consider adding that service for a while. It served my family well when my husband was dying; I didn't have to worry about missing a call from the doctor when someone else was on the line.
- Spending time with your friends is important. You may find your-self feeling guilty for being away, yet wanting to be with your friends. Carrie worked out this compromise when a family dinner with her dying mother conflicted with a party that she wanted to attend: she went to the dinner and enjoyed time with her family and relatives, but then excused herself so that she could catch up with her friends at the party, which she could now enjoy free of guilt.

7. WHO ELSE CAN YOU TALK TO?

As psychologists have been telling us for years, it helps to talk things out. Talking doesn't change the facts, but sharing problems with someone makes your load seem more manageable. What you don't want to do is hold your worries and concerns within yourself, sharing them with no one. Doing so will only make your ordeal worse.

What You Can Do

There are many resources available to you to help lighten the heavy emotional load that you may be carrying. School counselors are hired by the school system to be available to their students. What you share with them is confidential. They can even help if you find it difficult to talk to your parent or parents. Your priest, minister, or rabbi could be another resource. So could a trusted relative or family friend. Also, many mental-health centers have teen walk-in times. Find out the hours and go there. Take a friend with you if it is too scary to go alone (See topic 65; "What Happens When You See a Counselor?")

8. SUPPORT GROUPS

One of the significant developments that we have seen in recent years is the rise of support groups that provide emotional help to and from others in similar circumstances. They can be helpful in many ways. Those who attend find out that there are others who are struggling with like situations. It can be helpful to talk with people who truly understand what you are going through and who know how to cope with particular situations. Support groups can be like extended family. In fact, sometimes it is easier to talk there than at home. Support groups offer a safe place where one can say whatever is on his or her mind and know that no one will think it silly or ridicule it.

What You Can Do

Call your local hospice or mental-health center and ask whether they know of a group for teenagers. Check with your school counselor. If there isn't such a group yet, ask your school counselor or another adult to help you start one.

9. THE HOSPICE MOVEMENT

Another innovation of recent years is the hospice, which is an organization devoted to helping terminally ill persons endure pain and prepare themselves for death. The focus is on quality of life rather than quantity of life. Hospices help patients' families, too, as they can relieve them of the stress of being solely responsible for the care of a sick family member. Hospices also offer counseling to those who seek it, both before and after a death. Many support groups are sponsored by hospices.

What You Can Do

If your family has chosen to use the resources of a hospice to help your ailing loved one, you might initially feel some resentment because its services are such a strong reminder that your loved one is dying. You might feel that this amounts to giving up. But try to move beyond this. Make an effort to get to know the hospice worker that comes to your house. Look upon this person as someone you can talk to.

If the subject of hospice care hasn't come up, you might want to research the services available locally and provide this information to your parent or parents, who undoubtedly need all the help they can get during this difficult time.

10. FEELING SCARED

Are you feeling scared? If a loved one is dying, you have good reason to feel scared. Showing a brave front may be the macho thing to do, but we all know how many outward shows of bravado conceal genuine doubts and fears, like whistling when walking past the cemetery. The prospect of someone's death is very frightening to everyone. You're bound to be uncertain what your future will be like. What will graduation, weddings, and births be like without that person? Are there financial worries relating to this person's death? Will your family have to change its lifestyle? My children wondered if I would make enough money to support us. They had to abandon certain of their short-term aspirations. It was very scary for all of us.

What You Can Do

Talking things out is the best answer for all of these concerns. You are bound to be uncertain about some things, but there are others that are baseless and thus need not haunt you. Ask questions and get ideas about options by talking with adults in your family, friends, and possibly a teenage self-help group.

11. HOSPITAL VISITS

To anyone who has never visited one before, a hospital can be a strange, forbidding place. Add to this the prospect of seeing someone you love lying pale and vulnerable, perhaps in pain, possibly unconscious, and you have the ingredients for fear and apprehension. Yet, visits can be very comforting to all concerned. My dying husband didn't encourage our children to visit him at the hospital because it was so painful for him to be seen in such a helpless condition. I don't know that this was the best decision, but what he and they agreed upon was to visit with him on the telephone.

What You Can Do

- If you are planning your first visit to see a dying relative or friend, prepare for your visit by gaining some particulars on what you might see. How sick is the person? What hospital equipment will be in the room? What will it smell like? Will you see other sick people too? What does the person look like? Will the person recognize you? With information like this ahead of time, some of your anxiety should subside. Also, keep in mind that as the patient might tire easily, frequent short visits are often better than long ones.

- Keeping your loved one part of your life through hospital visits will help that person maintain his or her role in the family and continue to feel important. Just being there is reassuring, whether or not you talk a lot. Also, it's OK to take along some homework to do, or just to hang out. It might even be possible that your loved one could help you a bit, something that would make both of you feel good.

- There might be other things you could do, such as watching a ball game on TV, reading aloud a book or article of interest, or even a passage out of the Bible or Koran. Puzzles, cards, and other games provide more ways to spend time together. If the hospital allows it, decorating a nearby wall with a calendar, clock, colorful pictures, and cards will make the hospital room a more cheery place. Be creative. I know of two young people who taped pictures and clippings to the ceiling so the patient, lying flat on his back, could enjoy them better. (Better ask the nurses if this is OK.) These ideas work at home as well as in the hospital.

12. THE $64,000 QUESTION: AM I GOING TO DIE?

Something that might worry you in advance of that first hospital visit is the possibility that your loved one will ask you if you think he or she is going to die. This could be rather frightening, especially if you are not ready to deal with the subject yourself. First of all, you might not know the answer. Second, you might have great uneasiness about telling *that* to your loved one, assuming that you did know the answer. Would you really want to be the bearer of such news, particularly when you can't know what the patient's response will be? And how sure could you be that it was correct information, anyway?

What You Can Do

I have found that when someone says something really heavy to me and I don't know how to respond, I make a question out of their statement and ask it back. For example, a man asked me if he was going to die, so I in turn asked him, "What makes you think you are dying?" He went on to explain how he felt and what the doctors had told him. I never had to answer the question myself. You could use the same response if your loved one asked this $64,000 question of you. If pressed further, you could urge that he or she ask the doctor directly. After all, the doctor is the only person qualified to answer such questions.

13. HELPING YOUR SIBLINGS

If your family is struggling with a terminal illness, your parent or parents may be too preoccupied by ongoing events to pay much attention to the younger children. You yourself may wonder how much they know or should know. Thus, it might be up to you to give them the attention they need and to clue them in on the facts of the situation.

What You Can Do

Check with your parent or parents on what has been said and whether it would be OK for you to talk to them. Ask questions to get information on what they know. Try to answer questions as best you can, keeping in mind their age and maturity level. Simple, honest facts are best. If you don't know the answer to a particular question, say so and volunteer to consult with an adult.

14. FEELING ANGRY

Life isn't always fair. It's hard to understand why things happen as they do, and there are lots of things to be angry about. With many changes going on, you may feel that your life is out of control. You may be angry at the doctors who, you feel, are messing up, or you might be angry at your loved one for not taking better care of him- or herself.

What You Can Do

It's OK to be angry—but it isn't always OK to do what you do when you are angry. If anger is part of your grief, learn healthy, nonharmful ways of expressing it. (See topic 54, "Anger: Life Stinks; It's Not Fair.")

15. SAYING GOOD-BYE

Saying good-bye is a way we put an end to something and prepare to move on. It is a ritual we use constantly every day: we say good-bye whenever we leave the house to go to work or to school, for example. In a way, we are even saying good-bye when we tell our family good night as we get ready to go to sleep—ending one day, getting ready for the next. "See you in the morning," we add, subconsciously trying to assure ourselves that no calamity will occur while our loved ones sleep. When we tell our parents at the end of a telephone call, "I love you," we are really saying good-bye. These good-byes are relatively easy, because we see them as temporary.

Good-byes are more difficult when there is some degree of finality to them. When a friend moves to a different state or when a relationship breaks up, it's quite different from parting for a few hours or days. It is a sad and emotional time. You may recall such farewells, and remember the tears and sadness. What is true of other more-or-less final separations holds even truer when someone is dying. Just knowing that we can never see that person again makes parting doubly painful.

I don't like to tell people what to do. People are in charge of their own lives and must make their own decisions. But on this subject, I am going to come as close as I ever will to telling you what to do. And that is: If you have a chance, say good-bye!

What You Can Do

You might wonder how you can bring yourself to do this, for you might not even want to think about it because it makes the illness and prospect of death too real and too painful. But saying good-bye doesn't mean that you must be at the bedside when the person dies. You can say good-bye at any time during a person's illness and in many different ways. Start with thinking about things you want the ill person to know, things you have thought about but haven't told him or her. Think about what might be "unfinished" between the two of you. Organize your thoughts and then look for the opportunity or the time that feels right to talk about these things. If talking directly is too painful, write a letter, or make a cassette tape that you can give to your loved one.

It is common for people to give a gift to someone who is leaving, and dying is a final leave-taking. You might think of a gift that would have a special meaning between you and the person who is ill and may be dying. It need not be an expensive gift, but rather something you have made or written yourself—a part of you.

Saying good-bye can be as simple as saying "I love you" one more time. It might be an apology that needs to be expressed, or it might be a recalling of fond memories (as I did with my dad when he was dying), looking at pictures, discussing things you have learned from your loved one, or perhaps talking about your future plans. Special moments like these can help you feel more at peace when he or she dies. In a later chapter I will talk about how to say good-bye if death is sudden and there is no opportunity to say good-bye in the conventional way. (See topic 23, "When Death is Sudden," and topic 26, "No Time to Say Good-bye.")

16. SHOWING THAT YOU CARE

As you read these words, let us hope that your loved one will come through the crisis that brought you to this book. But if this is not to be, think about how you will feel when that person has died and you reflect on what you did or did not do during this time. How will you feel then? Will you regret not using the time that was left to show how much you cared? Or will you be able to say to yourself, "Thank goodness we were able to resolve those fights over early curfews and some of my friends. Thank goodness I was able to show Dad that I really loved him."

It may be hard to accept, but knowing in advance that a person is going to die presents loved ones with an opportunity that never comes in the case of sudden death. It is an opportunity to show that you care, possibly to remedy old differences, and to say good-bye. If you have that opportunity, you surely will want to take advantage of it—not just to show your loved one that you care, but also to prepare yourself for the day when that opportunity has passed.

What You Can Do

Your options will depend, of course, on your loved one's condition, but try to work out a schedule to be with him or her at least a few minutes every day to talk. This could even be in the morning before you go to school, if there won't be time later. Keep him or her informed on what is going on in your life. If talking is uncomfortable or difficult, you could work on a puzzle together, brush his hair, do her nails, or read aloud from a book or newspaper. Watch a TV show or listen to music together. Look for other activities and topics that you both can enjoy. And remind yourself how lucky you are to have the opportunity to do these things now.

Chapter 2

WHEN DEATH COMES

If you have been told that a loved one is dying and you are beginning to see that death is evident, your head might be spinning with questions that you're not comfortable asking anyone, especially if you don't know how others will react when you ask. What if I am the one who discovers that he has died? What will I see? Do I want to be there when she dies? What happens next? Who do I call? How do I break the news to Mom? To my sister? Where does the body go? What is death like to a dying person? What does a dead body look like? Feel like? Why do I feel so scared even thinking about it? It's important that you get answers to these questions to prepare you for what may lie ahead.

17. DISCOVERING THE BODY

It probably won't happen, but just in case you are the one to discover that your loved one has died, don't be surprised at the amount of shock you feel. Even though death is expected, it is still a shock to discover that it has actually happened. The image of what you have seen may stay with you for a while because of the trauma you have witnessed. If it was a long-anticipated death from natural causes, it probably won't last for more than a few days. But if it was a violent death, it could persist a long time and require you to seek professional counseling. (See topic 85, "What is Post-Traumatic Stress Disorder [PTSD]?")

What You Can Do

- As in every other aspect of life, it helps to prepare for what is to come. If you can, have a conversation with your parent or parents about this, or talk with the doctor, hospice worker, or home health nurse about what to expect at the time of death. What does death look like right after it happens? Are the eyes closed? Is the mouth open? What other physical changes might there be? The more you know about this, the less frightening it will be. It's the unknowns that make things the most scary.
- If you do discover the death of a loved one and it is a shocking discovery, seek out someone you can talk this out with, someone who really will listen to what you have to share and who does not try to change the subject or discourage you from relaying what you have seen. If the image haunts you, get professional help.

18. DO I WANT TO BE THERE WHEN HE DIES?

Perhaps the nurses or your parents are telling you that death is near. Do you want to be there? It might be very clear to you that you want to be there—or that you don't. Either way is OK. If it is a little too painful and scary to be there, take a walk or pray in a chapel. I remember a girl who told me that she wanted to be with her father when he died, but, at the same time, was afraid that she would be there. She was wrestling with the same ambivalence you might be struggling with.

What You Can Do

Once again, do not feel guilty if you don't want to be around when your loved one dies. You are not letting her down. It is important to go with your gut reactions and do what you think is best for you. I strongly trust people's instincts and support them. However, talk to your parents if you can, or to a trusted friend, and explain your feelings, explore how you might feel later, and gain the support that you need to put your mind at ease. Still, in the end, the decision is yours. I frequently have people tell me, after the fact, that they should have stayed—they feel somehow guilty for not being there at the time of death—and I give them support for their earlier decisions.

19. WHAT HAPPENS NEXT?

If the person dies in the hospital, the body is usually left in the room for a while so that family members can have some time to pray, say good-bye, or simply be alone with their loved one. Eventually, the body will be taken to a different part of the hospital called the morgue. There it will wait until a funeral director picks it up to take it to a funeral home, where it will be prepared for whatever is to follow, in accordance with the wishes of the family.

If your loved one dies at home, your hospice or home health worker or doctor can tell you who to call. A doctor will have to pronounce the person dead and sign a death certificate. This may seem strange to you, as it seems obvious that death has occurred, but that is the law. You may also be surprised to see that the time of death on the death certificate is probably different from when you know it to be. This happens because time will have elapsed between the actual death and the time that the doctor or coroner arrives to officially record it.

If death has occurred at home, you may or may not want to be there when the body is removed. Do what is best for you. It is hard to see a loved one being carried out of your home draped with a white cover or in a body bag—it seems so impersonal. A body bag is just that—an insulated bag for the safe transport of dead bodies.

What You Can Do

I can't say enough about asking questions and gathering information. The more you know about your concerns and questions, the easier it will be for you to make decisions on what is best for you. When you decide, let other family members know what you think, in order to avoid surprises later.

20. WHAT IS DEATH LIKE FOR THE DYING PERSON?

I am often asked, "What is death like for a dying person?" Don't we all wonder about that at times—not just about how others will die but about how we ourselves will die someday? I don't have an answer for that, but I do have some thoughts. Medicine today is such that, in most cases, people do not have to experience pain. People close to death have told me, "What I fear most is not knowing how I will die or how much pain I will have." One of the main goals of the hospice movement is to allow people to die pain-free. In many cases of terminal illness, people will begin to sleep more and more. It becomes more difficult to wake them for meals or to give them their pills, and they just sleep into death. In other cases, people might be frightened and restless, and can be calmed by music, prayers, and touch. (I once watched a mother stroke the head of her dying daughter and witnessed the daughter shift from restlessness into a calm, peaceful sleep.)

What You Can Do

The professionals involved in the care of your loved one might be able to give you information that will answer some of your questions. No one will know for sure, of course, but they can tell you what they have observed with other patients. Also, there are books that you can obtain at the library that have actual stories of people who have had close scrapes with death; the best known of these books is *Life After Life* by Raymond A. Moody Jr. Regardless of their scientific merit, these books are noteworthy in that they tend to be reassuring and not terrifying. Survivors often talk about being swept along a tunnel, seeing a wonderful bright light, feeling relaxed, and not wanting to return to this world. What I find remarkable is that these people say that they are no longer afraid to die. You might find a book like this helpful.

21. WHAT DOES A DEAD BODY LOOK OR FEEL LIKE?

When death occurs, a person's body will for a time look as though the person had just dropped off to sleep, or it might look very pale and very "dead." If a body has been dead for a few hours, you may notice bruiselike areas caused by the shutting down of blood circulation or muscular stiffness called *rigor mortis*. But don't be spooked by the presence of death; you can touch the body of your loved one if you want to. If death was recent, the body may still feel warm; otherwise, it will feel cool to the touch. If the body has been embalmed, the body will feel very firm as well as cool.

What You Can Do

Knowing in advance what to expect when your loved one dies should help you, at least a little, in getting through that painful experience. Knowing what to expect, you can decide in advance how you want to handle it.

22. WHY AM I SO WEAK AND JITTERY?

If weak and jittery is how you feel, let me assure you that *weak and jittery* is in fashion this season for people having to confront the death of loved ones. I expect that this is a pretty good description of how the adults in your family feel, too. A death can change so many things, leaving the future uncertain, and that is unnerving.

What You Can Do

You will feel better just acknowledging—to yourself and others—that your knees are shaking, your hands are trembling, or that you're feeling jittery. Think about the quarterback going into the fourth quarter trailing by three touchdowns. Is the game over? Not necessarily. Nervous energy can accomplish many things, including winning football games, and it can keep you going, too.

23. WHEN DEATH IS SUDDEN

Life is full of surprises and often not fair. The death of your loved one may not be one that you could plan and prepare for. It may be sudden, out of the blue, catching you off guard and totally overwhelming you. Even if the person was terminally ill, you might still be unprepared for the suddenness of it—perhaps death ultimately comes by way of a fall or fatal blood clot. The death might be caused by sudden illness, such as a heart attack or an aneurysm. Or your loved one might have been killed in an auto accident, a plane crash, a sailing mishap, or a mountain-climbing adventure turned deadly.

The death might have even been violent—murder, perhaps, or suicide. The shock of sudden death may leave your head pounding, your knees weak, your stomach upset, and your body overcome with emotion. Your mind may just go blank as you struggle to comprehend what you have just witnessed or heard.

What You Can Do

Talk, talk, talk. Talk it out of your system. Find people you can talk to about what has happened. Get family and friends together to share what has happened. Be together. Don't isolate yourself from the love and caring of family and friends. I know of occasions when close friends or relatives have simply moved in together to share in some terrible grief. You, too, will need others to share your grief. (See topic 50, "Responses to Expected Versus Sudden Death.")

24. HOW YOU FOUND OUT

How you found out about the death will play an important part in how you react to this news. Did a friend call you and, in the confusion of the moment, just drop the news into your lap? Did a policeman come to the door and invite you and your family to sit down, giving you a minute to mentally gear up for some bad news? Did your mother put her arms around you and begin by saying, "I love you so much, it hurts me to have to be the one to tell you. . . ." Or did you hear about the death in an even more traumatic way? Perhaps you went off to school expecting a regular day, only to be confronted at midmorning with "the news." Maybe you first heard it from a TV news report. This was how one family learned about the death of a son and brother killed in the Persian Gulf War. Another family came upon an accident on the road and immediately recognized the car as that of a family member. To their horror, they then learned that their loved one had died in the crash.

It seems that violence is increasing. Whether this is true, or whether it is just taking other forms, I don't know. Of late in this country, we have seen one example after another of school shootings—disturbed students shooting and killing their fellow students and teachers before the eyes of their peers. If you have witnessed such a horrific tragedy, or had a friend die in this senseless way, it will take longer than usual for you to recover.

Let me tell you about what is called post-traumatic stress disorder, or PTSD. Its symptoms might begin some weeks or even months after a traumatic event and might include flashbacks of what you experienced, or, if you weren't there, what you think it must have been like. There might be recurring nightmares, problems with sleeping, strong fears for your personal safety, a sense of doom, panic attacks, eating problems, and similar disruptions to your normal life. They might be present for a while and then go away, leaving you wondering if they will come again. If you are experiencing such symptoms or have had them in the recent past, and especially if they are interfering with your schoolwork, relationships both at home and at school, or your outside activities, don't keep them to yourself. Talk with your parents, if possible, or a teacher or even a close friend. Consult with your school counselor and get a referral, if he or she thinks it appropriate, to a therapist who can help you get your life back on track.

What You Can Do

To head off PTSD or lesser complications, talk about what you saw or imagined. Talking will help keep all those strong emotions from becoming internalized and creating problems for you. Talking with family, friends, school counselors, or anybody who will listen is extremely important in warding off future trouble. (See topic 85.)

25. I CAN'T BELIEVE THAT THIS HAS HAPPENED

Comprehending what has happened is going to take a lot longer when death is sudden than it would had death been expected and prepared for. You may feel very numb, devoid of any feeling, going through the day like a robot, dazed and out of touch. Some people tell me that they feel disconnected from what has happened, as if they were watching a play. They feel disassociated from everything and everybody.

What You Can Do

Once again, talking or writing about what has happened will not only help you, but it will help your friends and family as well. Talking will help you accept the reality of what has happened and help you begin to express your grief; it will keep this terrible event from being buried in your subconscious, whence it can create problems later. Talking will help those around you monitor your progress and, if necessary, get you the help you may need.

26. NO TIME TO SAY GOOD-BYE

Possibly the worst thing about sudden death is that it provides no opportunity to say good-bye—it leaves so many things just hanging, unsaid and unfinished. If you have had someone die this way, you are bound to revisit time and again the last contact you had with that person, the last words each of you said, the last expression on his or her face, the last smile, the last laugh, perhaps the last tear. We can hope that it was a happy encounter, but it might not have been. Perhaps you had an argument with your dad and stormed out the door, never thinking that this might be the last time you would see him alive. If your last experience with a loved one was anything like this, how terrible you must feel. How guilty. However, you cannot blame yourself for not knowing that there would never be an opportunity to apologize. Life is punctuated by such moments, and to suggest that one must never say or do anything that might call for a future apology is simply not realistic. Whenever anyone dies, there is always the feeling of wanting to tell him or her one more thing, whether it's an apology or a long-unsaid "I love you," but in sudden death those unsaid things multiply. If there were issues still unresolved at the time of death of your loved one—and if death was sudden, there are bound to be—that feeling, that need, that longing is going to be all the more intense.

What You Can Do

In chapter 1, "When Life Hangs in the Balance," we discussed the importance of saying good-bye. We will talk more about this in the next chapter, "Funerals, Formalities, and Farewells," as we explore ways that you can make a funeral or memorial service more meaningful for you. Here are some more ideas that may help.

You could write a letter to the person who died, saying everything that is important to you and asking all the questions you might have wanted to ask. If there is still time, that letter could be put into the coffin, or it could be taken and read at the grave site at any time. Or you could just put it into a safe place and reread it from time to time.

Another option is to obtain a biodegradable helium balloon, write messages on it or attach notes to it, take it outside, and let it rise to the heavens. (Avoid mylar or microfoil, which endanger sea life.) When I do this with my teen groups, the messages are personal and not shared with one another (unless a teen wants to share a message). Deciding how we are going to let the balloon go is always a nice part of the preparation. If you decide that this is something that you would like to do, you can also decide with whom you want to do it—your family, your friends, whatever group is most meaningful to you. And as you prepare to release the balloon you might want to develop a ritual of your own. Do you want to sing a song, read a poem, share your messages with one another, or just count one, two, three and release?

Corny as it may seem, that little balloon ceremony has proven to be very popular with grieving people of all ages because it is such a visual representation of their desire to reach out to their loved ones, to communicate their love across the vastness of space and, at the same time, to literally and figuratively let go. If you have such a ceremony, you are likely to be left with a sense of peace and quiet when it's over. And don't be surprised if everyone present becomes very quiet, each deep in his or her thoughts about the person who has died, perhaps quietly crying, letting some of the sadness escape.

When a sister-in-law of mine died some years ago, at a time when neither my children nor I could attend the funeral a long distance away, one of my grown daughters came to my house with a balloon and said, "We need to tell Aunt Keck goodbye." We then wrote many messages to her and also included some for her to give to my daughter's dad, who had died when she was just thirteen. We took the balloon to an open space and launched it. It felt good and gave us a nice opportunity to continue sharing our memories of this departed friend and relative as the afternoon passed.

27. DO YOU WANT TO KNOW THE DETAILS?

When death is sudden and possibly traumatic, do you want to know the circumstances of what happened? How much detail do you want to know? You may not have had a choice about the initial news; a newspaper or television report might have caught you off guard. Even though the authorities and news organizations try to prevent the premature disclosure of victims' identities, this is not always possible. And when such news does break, harmful and inaccurate rumors often get started. They can be painful. If you are having to wrestle with such rumors, my advice is to ask your parents or other responsible persons to track down the most reliable information they can. Avoid getting caught up in speculation, which can be terribly upsetting and have no foundation in fact.

What You Can Do

- As quickly as you can, let your family and friends know where you stand on how much you want to know. Commonly, parents and friends will give out only basic information, not knowing how much the person wants to hear. So, it is up to you to ask questions when you feel ready to hear the answers. If you suspect that you are hearing only rumors, find out who would have correct information. In order to counter the spread of falsehoods, it is important to identify what is only rumor and what is fact.
- Be aware that the more violent the death, the more unpleasant the details might be. Airplane crashes, car accidents, murders, and suicides are seldom free of disturbing images. If a loved one or dear friend has died in such circumstances, you should decide how much detail you want to have. You know, better than anyone else does, what you can endure.

I hope for you that you are not having to deal with truly grim news, but if you are and it is proving too hard to deal with, find a family member, counselor, clergyman, or therapist to talk to.

28. FLASHBACKS OR NIGHTMARES

It is hard to put traumatic events out of your mind. You can keep busy, which will help keep you from focusing on them, but they will always be in your subconscious. The memory of what has happened may come out when you least expect it, taking the form of flashbacks or dreams—mental pictures of what happened or of what you perceive happened. These can be very disturbing and often interfere with schoolwork, relationships, and life in general.

What You Can Do

- Understand that this sort of thing happens to people all the time. If it's happening to you, don't be alarmed. But do find someone who you can share this with, someone who can give you some help. Sharing flashbacks or nightmares is like being able to give away part of your stress, making the burden lighter and more manageable. If you do not find immediate relief, seek out professional help. (See topic 65, "What Happens When you See a Counselor?")
- Keeping a diary is one way to get control of these things. You can keep your record in a notebook or, if you have a computer, record it in a computer file. Describe the content of your flashbacks or nightmares, take note of the dates that they occur, and record how long they last. This will give you, and perhaps your therapist, a clear idea of whether they are getting worse or beginning to wear off. (For more on dreams see topic 76, "Dreams and Nightmares.")

29. WHEN YOU CAN'T CRY

Adults as well as teens have often told me that they can't cry. The tears just aren't there, they say. This is a normal reaction to severe emotional pain, rather like the numbness that occurs when struck a hard blow. I know a man who, as a young sailor, dropped a porthole cover on his head. He tells me that he required no anesthesia as a doctor stitched up the wound—he couldn't feel a thing! Emotional blows can have the same effect.

There are other reasons why you might not be able to cry: You might have too much to do taking care of others to think about what has happened or what it means for your future. You might be holding back tears because you fear that your tears will get everyone else started—and that would be too much to bear. You might be restrained by well-meaning family members or friends who are telling you to be strong and making you feel that tears are a sign of weakness. (Unconsciously, perhaps, they might be protecting themselves from the sight of you crying.) But tears are not a sign of weakness. Just the opposite—we gain strength from crying, letting the feelings out. Everyone feels better after a good cry; you might say that's why crying was invented!

It's possible that you know all of this, and yet still find that you cannot let go and have a good cry. You may even wonder if family and friends will think that you didn't care enough for the person who died. Sometimes that numbness I spoke about simply won't let the tears come out.

What You Can Do

- In cases of sudden death, it often happens that people find the shock so great that all feelings are numbed out, and they simply cannot cry. Crying in this case may start weeks later. I have no magic formula to turn on your tears, but if you are unable to cry right now, you can take some comfort just knowing that this is very common and that your tears undoubtedly will come when you're ready for them.
- You might also look for a catalyst to help the tears get started. This could be something as simple as watching a sad movie or reading a sad book. Writing poetry or a letter to the deceased may also help the tears start to flow.

- When my first husband died—and it was after a long illness, not sudden—I wasn't able to cry for a time. Since then, I have learned how healthy it is to cry and can cry whenever I feel sad about something. My advice on this score is absolutely unequivocal: If you feel tears coming, let them flow. If people are uncomfortable with your tears, that is their problem.

- Must you cry? Is it possible to grieve without crying? Human beings have different emotional patterns, and it may be that some people can go through the grieving process without tears. But my guess is that even when this happens, it is because they are fighting back the tears. And why? What is the point? We have the historic scenes of the Kennedy family stoically going through the painful ceremonies following President Kennedy's assassination, but of course they cried in private. Crying is a natural release of emotions that need to be discharged.

Chapter 3

FUNERALS, FORMALITIES, AND FAREWELLS

Here comes the subject I least want to talk about, you're probably thinking. This is the adult world telling me that I have to go through a horrible ceremony because my loved one died. Why do my family and friends and I have to endure such a gloomy ritual?

I do understand your revulsion at the thought of having to put your sorrow on display for all to see. But is that really all there is to a funeral? Let's think about it.

30. WHY DO WE HAVE FUNERALS?

Why do we have funerals? Well, for one thing, they are the last caring thing we can do for our loved one. Second, they provide a way to show respect for that person and his or her life. We don't simply dispose of the body; a funeral is a way of saying how important that person was to us. Third, they give us a way to say good-bye. Fourth, they provide others— friends and relatives—an opportunity to express their sorrow, offer support, and to say good-bye themselves. And, finally, they help confirm for us, subconsciously, what has happened: that our loved one really has died. It is a way of bringing down the curtain on his or her life, giving some semblance of order to its last act.

31. BUT WHAT IF IT HURTS TOO MUCH?

That's all well and good, you may be saying. But your pain is so great that you don't see how you could bring yourself to do *anything* right now. Do you really have to do all this? No, you don't have to. Must you go to the wake, if there is one, or attend the funeral, if there is one, or sit shiva? No. You can sit in your room and feel sorry for yourself. But I think that you will want to participate at least a little bit in these preparations and in the rituals themselves, not just out of love and respect for the person who died, but out of concern for how you will feel when it's all over. I know too many people who chose not to attend and *deeply regret it now.*

To a surprising extent, if you think about it, our lives really are framed by ceremonies and rituals of one kind or another. For the most part, these special occasions are happy times: births, baptisms, birthdays, holidays, confirmations, bar and bat mitzvahs, graduations, weddings, awards ceremonies, anniversaries. On all such occasions we invite family and friends to share in the joy.

Funerals are the same idea in reverse. Instead of joy, what we share is pain and sorrow. And yet it is important that this pain and sorrow be expressed, by you and everyone else who is grieving the death of your loved one. Gathering together to express your grief, to show your love, and to celebrate, in a way, that person's life is the first step toward the healing that you all need. And that is what funerals are all about.

What You Can Do

To make it easier for you to decide on the level of your participation in these events, ask your parents, or someone you trust, what will be happening and what is expected of you. Ease into it by playing some small role in planning the events to make them as meaningful as possible to yourself.

32. HELPING YOURSELF BY GETTING INVOLVED

It may be hard for you to accept right now, but having things to do in preparing for a funeral will actually help you endure your pain. There was a time years ago—and this continues today in simpler societies—when families would wash and dress the body, construct the casket, and dig the grave. Now funeral directors attend to such matters. Thank goodness, you may be saying! But you and your family will surely want to select the clothing to be worn, plan the funeral service, decide about cremation or burial, select a burial site, provide the information needed for newspaper stories about your loved one, and provide the funeral director with a photo that can guide him or her in preparing the body for viewing, if that is appropriate.

Think about the music for a minute. I'm sure that the person who died had certain music that he or she loved, and I'm sure you do, too. Wouldn't you like to have some of that music included in the funeral service?

I recently met with a mother and her seventeen-year-old daughter. I was told that the girl's dad, the woman's husband, had a favorite song that he hummed, sang, and whistled year-round: the Christmas carol "Silent Night." So, at the daughter's request, as people were starting to leave the church at the end of the funeral service, the organist struck up "Silent Night." People smiled as they joined in singing this beautiful carol. Then, as the family emerged from the church, the minister greeted them by continuing to play the carol on his trumpet. This little personal touch closed the service in a very positive way, breaking the somber mood and helping people feel closer to one another and to the deceased.

You are bound to have all sorts of things you would want said about your loved one. You could suggest that certain people be asked to speak about their memories of the deceased. Or possibly you might be able to muster the strength to speak yourself. If not, perhaps you could write something for someone else to read.

Of course, there are many other things to be done after someone dies—calling relatives and friends, arranging for sleeping accommodations for those from out of town, and planning a reception for friends and relatives after the funeral among them. All of this is hard to think about, I know, but I believe that you will find that participating in some of these duties is a way of releasing your tension and mourning your loss.

What You Can Do

- All grief is personal. No one can tell you how you must, or must not, grieve. The decision to participate in funeral planning, in a wake, or a funeral itself should be yours to make. Still, I cannot emphasize enough how important it will be to you in future years that you participate in these rituals in some way to express your love and respect to your own satisfaction. Generally, what that means, hard as it may be, is that you play some part in planning and carrying out these painful ceremonies.

- If for some reason, such as being hospitalized, you didn't attend the funeral, perhaps the service could be taped or recorded in some fashion so that you could see it or hear it later. (See topic 72, "When You Can't Attend the Funeral.")

- If you decide that there is no way you can attend the funeral, you should consider going to the funeral home and privately visiting the body of your loved one. (Doing this with a family member you feel especially close to, not alone, is probably a good idea.) Seeing the body of the person who died will give you a chance, very privately, to say good-bye, and will help you come to acknowledge, subconsciously, that this person really has died. However, if the body has been badly scarred, perhaps in an accident, it may not be possible to view the body and you will have to think of other ways to say your goodbye. (See topic 26, "No Time to Say Good-bye.")

- If the funeral has already occurred and you didn't attend, there is still something you could do to show your love and respect, and that is to carry out a private, symbolic burial of your own. (See topic 35, "Memorial Services.")

33. THE VIEWING, VISITATION, OR WAKE

Now we come to the least-understood of these sad ceremonies—the viewing, visitation, or wake—a customary practice in some religious traditions, but not others. What are we talking about? Regardless of the name, this is an informal gathering of friends and relatives, either at a funeral home or a church, where people can visit the body of the person who died and express their sorrow and sympathy. It is usually held in the afternoon or evening a day or two before the funeral or memorial service. If you and your family have such a gathering, there may be some family or friends who prefer to attend this rather than the funeral, because it will be less formal and give them a chance to talk in a more relaxed way. Others, because of their own schedules, may not be able to attend the funeral but can come for this gathering.

The "viewing" may be just that: an opportunity to view the deceased for one last time. Usually, the casket is open, but the family could decide against an open casket and instead place a picture of the person who died on the closed casket. This might be because the body was damaged in an accident or there had been a long, disfiguring illness preceding death. Or the family simply might decide that it didn't want an open casket, wanting people to be left instead with the memory of how that person looked in life. My children and I decided not to have the casket open for their father, following a remark he had made long before: "If I ever die, I don't want people looking at me in a casket." I had remembered that comment and discussed it with my children, and we agreed to follow his wish.

However, sometimes you have to compromise. My husband's parents lived over 1,200 miles from us, and they needed to see his body and to say their goodbyes. To accommodate them we had a short, family-only viewing just before the scheduled funeral service.

What You Can Do

- As you think about it, what would you like to do? Let the adults know your ideas and how you feel. But keep in mind that where many people are involved, some compromises may have to be made. It is always useful to have a "plan A" and a "plan B." Thus, if your first idea is shot down, you will have a backup idea to avoid feeling so rejected.
- If you are so inclined, you might want to assemble for display at the viewing a collage of pictures depicting the life of the person who died—as a child, as a young bride or bridegroom, as a mother or father. Or you could put together a slide show of scenes from his or her life that could be shown at the viewing or later at the reception at home.
- If you would like to remind people of special things about your loved one, you could suggest special floral displays such as those we had at my father's viewing. My father was a farmer, so for that occasion, the florist prepared several beautiful floral displays incorporating various symbols of my father's life: toy tractors, Hereford cattle, and horses. Also, because my father loved the wildflowers that grew on his land, his grandchildren collected bouquets of them to add to the more formal arrangements. You might want to do something similar: it is ideas like this that can make such an event a celebration of life rather than death.
- Be prepared to receive a lot of hugs, which sometimes have more meaning than words. While this can be a lovely experience, it can also be strange. Remember, the hugs come from a place of love, so try to be gracious.

- Be prepared for a lot of "I'm so sorry your dad has died." But don't feel that you must think of things to say in response. All you have to say is a simple "Thank you."
- And—this may surprise you—be prepared for laughter as people share memories and stories. It is bound to come as people recall the highlights of this life that has ended. Listen to these stories and you may hear things that you didn't know, wonderful stories that will become treasures for you and provide an opportunity to get to know your loved one on a different level. You can learn what his coworkers thought about him or her, achievements you didn't know about, or the sense of humor that you didn't see. I remember that some parents were astonished to learn that their teenage son had made a habit of stopping by a local nursing home after school to visit with the old people there. They had never known that before. How wonderful to find that out, even after he died.
- If you feel that you need some fresh air during the viewing, let someone know where you are going and take a friend with you. Don't go out alone.

34. SITTING SHIVA

Earlier in this chapter I used the term *sit shiva*. Jewish readers will recognize this term, but non-Jewish readers might not be familiar with it. Sitting shiva is a wonderful practice that provides an opportunity for relatives and friends to visit the home of the grieving family and express their condolences in the days after the funeral. Traditionally, this has been seven days, but it may be as short as three days.

What You Can Do

- If you are Jewish, your family will most likely want to sit shiva after the funeral. Painful as it may be to see anyone or to go through any of the rituals of death, sitting shiva can be very comforting to you and your loved ones.

- If a Jewish friend has died, the two or three days before the funeral may not be appropriate times for you to reach out to the family, but after the funeral you should ask if the family will be sitting shiva. Depending on your relationship to the family, your visit can be earlier or later in the period. The first day or two usually are for relatives and the family's closest friends.

- Caring gestures need not be limited to shiva. After shiva, when friends and family have gone, is a time when a gesture of friendship may be most appreciated.

35. MEMORIAL SERVICES

What is the difference between a funeral and a memorial service? A standard funeral service usually takes place about two or three days after a death and is conducted with the body present. Unlike a funeral service, a memorial service can be held at any time one chooses after the death—even months later. Of course, the body is not present. The service can be held in a church, a synagogue, a funeral home, a hall, or any place large enough to hold the expected number of people. Sometimes the memorial service is the public event that follows a private, family-only funeral. You and your family could choose some person to officiate, perhaps a minister, priest, or rabbi, or simply a friend or family member. This might be a less-formal service where different people could be asked to speak or read a letter or a poem that was significant to the person who died.

Even if you have had a formal funeral service, you and your family might still want to have a memorial service later. Such was the case when a beloved high school teacher died. The students felt there needed to be something more and planned a memorial service at their school gym. The planning and execution of this service was very healing to these students and helped them express their grief and get on with their lives.

What You Can Do

- As with the funeral planning, make sure that your family knows how you think and feel regarding the memorial service.
- You may want to participate in the memorial service by writing something or finding an appropriate passage in some literary work to either read yourself or have someone read for you. This is an opportunity to be creative, to make the service a celebration of your loved one's life and not so much an acknowledgment of her death. If you can contribute to this result, you will feel good about it, and those present will leave feeling uplifted.
- Once again, if you feel overwhelmed by all the people, noise, and hugs, you can slip out for a few minutes or take a walk with a friend—but be sure to let someone know. A memorial service might go on for a few hours, and you can reappear in a few minutes or so. You may need some time just to process all that has happened.

36. THE BURIAL SERVICE

Talk about finality! When you bury somebody in the ground, that's finality! Are you ready for this? Who is?

It's hard, very hard, to think about putting the body of someone you love in the ground. And yet, there are only two choices, burial or cremation, when someone has died. Painful as it is to address, you and your family will have to decide on one or the other if no instructions have been left. You may want to think about what you would be most comfortable (or least uncomfortable) with and share your thoughts with your parent or parents.

If the choice is burial, you might have some ideas about which cemetery to choose. You might even want to ride along when the adults select the site. Keep in mind that the site your family chooses may not only be a resting place for your loved one, but in future years other family members may be buried there as well.

My children and I had a very serious decision to make when their father died: whether to bury him in Virginia, where we were living, or back in his childhood home in Minnesota, where his parents and other relatives still lived. If we buried him in Virginia and then decided to move back to Minnesota, what would we do with his body? Furthermore, his parents had already selected a burial site near those of other family members. After thinking this through, we decided to take his body back to Minnesota for burial in the family plot. This meant, of course, that cemetery visits for us would be rare as long as we remained in Virginia.

If your family should choose a similarly distant site, making cemetery visits difficult, you might suggest designating some special spot in a park, or even the backyard, where you could go to meditate or think about your loved one.

Dealing with these kinds of questions is a way of mourning your loss.

I'm sure that you know generally about funeral processions—those long lines of cars with their headlights on, heading toward a cemetery somewhere. Always sad to see, always sobering; the exception would be those Dixieland jazz funerals in New Orleans, where musicians in tuxedos lead the parade with rousing music. Most likely, though, your family will decide on something more conventional, and you will ride together to the cemetery. There won't be any horn solos.

When you arrive at the cemetery, there will probably be a short service at the graveside. Perhaps a minister will say a few more words about your loved one. When he finishes, people can leave. It's for you and your family to decide, but, depending on your religion, you may wish to have the casket lowered into the ground later. In Jewish ceremonies, the casket is lowered as part of the graveside service and family members are given an opportunity to participate by picking up handfuls of dirt to place in the grave, symbolizing the return of the body to dust, emphasizing finality, and helping them with closure.

Once the burial is complete, it is customary for the bereaved family to invite friends, neighbors, and relatives to their home, the home of a close friend, or a church dining room to share refreshments or a meal. This may include food that has been prepared and donated by friends and neighbors, also a universal custom.

Hard as it may be to believe, you and your family will probably feel a certain sense of relief when the funeral and burial have ended. Once again, you may hear people laughing, as well as crying, as they share stories and memories.

What You Can Do

- Because it is painful to think of your loved one down in the ground, I suggest that you remind yourself of the basics of what it is to be dead. Your loved one will never breathe, never eat, never see, never feel again. What you knew and loved was not a body; it was the spirit, the personality, the wonderful combination of traits that make up a living person. Sadly, that is gone. All that is left is the shell in which it dwelled. It is only the shell that will occupy that grave; the person you knew lives on in memory.
- Bring extra tissues with you, for your own tears as well as those of others.
- Don't be surprised to find that you don't want to leave the burial site, feeling that you are leaving your loved one all alone in a strange place. You may be aware that this is the last thing you can do for your loved one. This is it! It's all over! Having a

special friend or favorite relative with you can help you get through this part.

- Going back to join friends and relatives at a reception will help take the heaviness out of the day. You may even find yourself enjoying your friends, making plans for going back to school, and—don't feel guilty—laughing at a joke. Your grief will continue to thread in and out of your life as time goes on.

37. VISITING THE GRAVE

Visiting the grave at least once after the burial is important. It can be frightening, but once you do it, it should be less scary. Phyllis, for example, wanted to visit the grave of her mother, but her dad was resisting. He wasn't ready yet, and he felt that he was protecting her. She was able to drive, and she wanted to go there by herself. We met in my office to look at alternatives and came up with a plan. I felt that it probably would be all right for Phyllis to visit the grave by herself, but I was concerned about how difficult it might nevertheless turn out to be. If she became very upset, it might be dangerous for her to drive home. We decided that Phyllis and her dad should go together, but that her father would stay in the car parked near the cemetery and Phyllis could walk in alone, spend whatever time she needed, and return to her dad waiting in the car. She could take a friend if she wanted to. After the visit, she and her dad and friend would stop somewhere for a snack and conversation if that felt right. Phyllis also knew that it might take her dad a few days even to work up to this plan, but that was fine with her, and he ultimately agreed to it.

What You Can Do

- Communicating your thoughts, feelings, and wishes is important. Even though at times it may seem that your parents can read your mind, they really can't. It will help you to remember that they are caught up in their own grief, too, and that they may not be aware of your needs. As you express your wishes, stay flexible and try to understand your parents' feelings. Being willing to negotiate plans that suit everybody will serve you well not only in these circumstances but throughout your life.

• Visits to the grave site need not be long ones. Five or ten minutes is often long enough. Think about what you want to do there. Do you want to leave a flower, read a note or a poem, play some music? Make your visits meaningful to you.

38. CREMATION

Cremation is the other choice you and your family have in disposing of the body. Burn your loved one's body? Is that what we're talking about? The idea of cremation can be frightening because fear of fire is a basic human trait. Also, most people don't know just what happens during cremation, and, anyway, it is hard to think of destroying the precious body of a loved one.

Why would someone choose cremation over burial? For one thing, it costs less. And it takes up less space in an increasingly crowded planet. Then there is the option of having one's ashes scattered somewhere that has special meaning for that person—the mountains, say, or seashore. I would prefer this myself, but if my family prefers a regular burial, that's all right with me. After all, I'll be dead, and funerals and memorial services are really for the living.

Knowing a little bit about the cremation process may be helpful. In this country, the body is not set on fire. The funeral director will take the body to the "crematory," which is a kilnlike oven lined with firebrick. There, the body is heated to a very high temperature, causing it to be reduced to ashes. The ashes are then gathered up and put into a cardboard box or an urn, which is simply a decorative container.

If your family decides on cremation, you might have some ideas on what to do with the ashes. Some people bury them in a grave or a columbarium, which is a wall in a mausoleum with niches into which the urn can be placed. Other people are comfortable having the ashes of loved ones in their homes, up on a mantel or on a shelf in the closet. Your family might even consider scattering the ashes in one or more places having significance to your loved one. The possibilities are numerous, and the choice will be up to you and your family.

What You Can Do

- Knowing what the process and choices are, you will have a better idea of what you would like—or maybe you don't want any part of this decision. Either way, that's OK. Think it through and let your family know your thoughts.
- You do not have to use the container or urn furnished by the funeral home. If you have a lovely vase, or even a nice box, that can be used instead.

39. THE HEADSTONE

If the decision is for burial, the headstone marking the grave is another opportunity to show your love for the person who died. I like it when I see a headstone that tells me something about the person who is buried there. For instance, I was in a cemetery recently and saw a tractor etched on a headstone, immediately telling me that this was the grave of a farmer. I'm sure that that gentleman would have been pleased to be so identified.

In some cemeteries, the type of headstone is determined for you. The choices are few: name, date of birth, date of death. In others, there will be many choices to make: the shape of the headstone or monument, the color of stone, or maybe no stone at all but a metal plaque.

With all of the other decisions to be made, however, I would say that the choice of a headstone is a decision that can be put off. Many people delay this, not only because they need time to think about it, but also because it represents an additional cost that they want to defer.

I do want to warn you, though, that once a headstone is in place, visiting the grave can be a shock. Seeing the name of your loved one with a birth and death date etched in granite is powerful. It will again drive home the reality of the death.

What You Can Do

- You could start this process by coming up with some ideas, such as a few words that describe the personality or philosophy of your loved one, or perhaps some poetry or verse that he or she loved.
- You might suggest a family meeting where people could express their ideas and preferences. If you can stand it, perhaps a visit to a cemetery to see what other people have done would give all of you a starting point.

Chapter 4

UNDERSTANDING YOUR GRIEF

If you are grieving a terrible loss, you may be wondering what's happening to you. You may be in a kind of daze, lost in your sorrow and not knowing what tomorrow will bring. You may feel that you are losing your mind.

If this even comes close to how you're feeling right now, it will help you to know that others your age have been where you are today, suffering more or less alone the painful adjustments that the loss of a loved one can bring. It will also help if you can identify the feelings that are surging through you; a feeling that you can name loses some of its power in the naming. It will help you to feel more normal. Remember, you are *not* losing your mind. You're *grieving*.

40. WHAT IS GRIEF? WHAT IS MOURNING?

You know it when you feel it, but what is grief, anyway? It is variously defined as "intense mental anguish" or "keen mental suffering." Simply put, it's the feeling you have when you experience an important loss. In other words, it's *what's to be expected* when you suffer a loss. As you read this book and come to understand grief more, you will realize that people can expect to endure this deep sadness many times in their lives, but, fortunately, not always with the same intensity. For example, when you graduate from high school, you may be happy, but just the same, you are leaving a part of your life, never to return, and you're likely to feel a deep sadness as well. Or think back to the time you broke up with a boyfriend or a girlfriend. Did it hurt? Did you have strong feelings? I'll bet you did! Well, you were grieving. *Any* important loss you suffer in your life is likely to bring with it a certain sense of grief.

When you are grieving, you have feelings that need to be expressed. By "expressed," I mean that you have to let other people know how you're feeling and, what is even more important, satisfy your own need to *do something*. This is what we call *mourning*.

I don't have to tell you that there are both good and bad ways to mourn. For the sake of your own mental and physical well-being, it is important to mourn your loss in a way that you will feel good about when you think back to this time in your life.

What You Can Do

Get the facts! Inform yourself not only about the subject of your grief but about grief itself. Not knowing what's going on can be frightening and frustrating. Knowing what people go through in their grief, you will encounter fewer surprises and will be better able to deal with things as they happen. You will also have a better understanding of what others—family members and friends—may be going through.

41. HOW LONG IS GRIEF?

How long is grief? I am often asked this question by grievers and nongrievers alike. Parents, for example, sometimes wonder when their daughter will return to "normal." The answer I give is that grief takes *as long as it takes*. It will definitely take longer than three months, and it could take several years. I'm not sure we ever get over grief, but I do know you will get past this pain that you're feeling now and will be able to look back and once again enjoy memories of the person who died. The loss you have endured will get integrated into your life as time passes. Keep in mind that we are who we are. We are molded by life's experiences, and each of us is a unique collection of good, bad, happy, and sad experiences.

As you read through this book, you will find that there are many aspects to grief. It isn't something simple that can be wrapped up in a neat package. Throughout your life, you are likely to revisit your grief many times. At unexpected times, particularly when there is an important event in your life, you may be reminded of your loss. I don't mean that you will go back through this heavy pain that you are experiencing now, but you may feel a deep sense of sadness, a wistfulness, and regret that this person you love cannot share some event with you. I have seen this in my children throughout the years. For example, when one of my daughters was breaking up with her husband, I noticed pictures of her late father suddenly appearing in her bedroom. It told me that she wished that she might have the help and comfort he could have provided, had he lived. I don't know how long your intense grief will take, but it will help you endure it if you have some idea of what is going on inside you and inside those around you.

What You Can Do

The more you work at identifying your feelings and then expressing them, the better off you will be. Feelings denied or bottled up won't stay bottled up forever; they will only come out later to haunt you. They will return when you least expect it in the form of emotional flare-ups or physical ailments. My advice is to learn to understand what you are feeling and to have patience with yourself. Grief takes a long time and can't be rushed. Understanding yourself will enable you to help your loved ones and help yourself, too.

42. AM I NORMAL?

Am I normal, you ask? Probably! This is a question I get asked a lot, not only from teens, but adults as well. Grief is different for everybody. Maybe you can already see that in your immediate family: you might see one member very angry, another person expressing guilt, and another seemingly getting along just fine. What this should tell you is not that you are abnormal, but that everyone's grief is unique. Here is why:

- Each of you had a certain, specific relationship to the person who died. The survivor who was closest to the deceased may be feeling the greatest sense of loss, but the person who had a conflicted relationship with the deceased—perhaps their last meeting was a big fight—may have to deal with more guilt. If you did not even know or like the person who died, you may feel no grief at all. In that case, you should know there is no such thing as a duty to grieve, although there is a duty to respect the grief of others.
- Grief is different for each of us because we all cope differently. You may have learned excellent ways to cope as you were growing up. Those coping skills will be helpful to you now. Not everybody is so lucky. Or, your parents may have set an example of coping that is not healthy—using drugs, drinking, acting hatefully toward each other. In either case, just keep in mind that *you are in charge*. Even if your parents have not prepared you for grief, you can change how you cope now. You can grow through this if you want to. You can become a better, more understanding person. Your life can be richer.
- The circumstances around the death will also influence your grief. Was it an expected death or was it a sudden, violent

death? Was your loved one ill for many months or, as with my children's father, years? Did he die suddenly or violently? How did you find out about the death? Did you have a chance to say good-bye? None of these things can be changed, of course, but it will help you to know how they can affect the intensity of your grief. (See chapter 8, "Tightening the Screws.")

• Your grief will be affected, as well, by what else is going on in your life. You may have had to put it on hold because of other matters taking priority. For example, the week that you return to school after attending your brother's funeral may be exam week, which could force you to put your grief in the back of your mind so that you can focus on the task at hand. That's OK—you will deal with the grief later. But you can't escape it; it's still there.

What You Can Do

Resources are available to help you, but it's up to you to take advantage of them. Books, support groups, lectures, and the Internet are there. People who seek out and use resources available to them usually manage their grief better and more easily.

43. WHO AM I? I FEEL DIFFERENT

I remember a girl who longed to be identified as she once was, as the popular girl who was a cheerleader and editor of her school newspaper, for she felt that her identity had changed to "the girl whose brother killed himself." When a loved one dies, you may find yourself more sensitive to comments and glances than you were before. Things that used to roll off your back now hurt, leaving you to wonder what people "really meant" or if their looking uncomfortable means that they have been talking about you.

When a loved one dies, you may find that your identity has somehow changed. You may now be an only child if a sibling dies; you may now live in a single parent home. You may be an orphan if both of your parents were killed in an accident. How do you answer questions regarding your family when an important person is missing? You might find yourself trying to take the place of the loved one who has died, like the girl who felt that she had to be the social stand-in for her deceased mother, making an effort to look, dress, and sound like her, or the boy who felt that he had to follow in his deceased brother's footsteps so that his parents wouldn't be so sad.

What You Can Do

If you fear answering questions about members of your family, spend some time thinking of different responses that you might want to have ready for different situations. There are times when you may want to say, "I have two sisters, but one has died," or you may want to say, "I have one living sister" and leave it at that. As long as you have rehearsed some responses to dreaded or expected questions, you won't be caught off guard and uncomfortable. You might suggest that other family members do this as well.

Finally, think about this for a minute. A void has been created by this death, and it is a natural impulse to try to fill voids. You may be thinking that somehow you have a duty to replace the person who died. This is *not* your job: your job is to focus on your *own* uniqueness, on your own kind, wonderful self. If you're not even sure who you are right now, spend some time thinking about yourself and ask yourself questions like: What is there about me that's special? What do I stand for? What do I believe? What do I look for in friends? What are my goals in life? What are people likely to find interesting in me? What can I do to become a better person?

As you do this, avoid assigning to the person who died superhuman qualities that you can't hope to match. Since we are all imperfect, your loved one no doubt had some weaknesses along with his or her strengths. You probably have different strengths and weaknesses. You can't be that other person, but you can be yourself.

Another way to do this exercise is to put together a collage about yourself. Get some old magazines and start cutting out words and pictures that will tell the story of who you are. You might even invite family or friends to join you. They might be surprised to find out things about you that they never knew before.

44. I CAN'T SLEEP

If you are having trouble sleeping, it might seem that nature has decreed bedtime to be the time for thinking. You get all settled in, looking forward to a good night's sleep, and as soon as you turn off the light, your mind turns on. Thoughts come into your head, you start thinking about what has happened, and you may even start to cry. You toss and turn into the early-morning hours. The alarm goes off at six o'clock, and you find that you have had only four hours of sleep. On top of that, you have an exam at school—definitely not a good way to start the day or to cope with your grief. Grief in itself is exhausting, and you need sleep.

What You Can Do

You need your rest! Here are some ways to help yourself get that rest.

- Have a glass of warm milk or chamomile tea before you go to bed, as these are known to be natural sedatives. Avoid chocolate, coffee, or black tea because they contain caffeine.
- Try some meditation to quiet your mind. Look for relaxation tapes that you can borrow from the library.
- Is the beach one of your favorite places? There are devices available now that emit ocean sounds that will remind you of happy

times and soothe you. There are other choices, too, including rain, a babbling brook, a summer night, or sounds of the woods.

- Soft easy-listening music may lull you to sleep. (Remember, I said "soft and easy.")
- Try a warm bath or shower. Maybe aromatherapy or deep breathing will help too.
- Be sure to exercise early in the day—late-day workouts can get you wound up.
- And then, perhaps, some light reading or a movie may put you right to sleep.

45. WHAT ABOUT DREAMS?

Dreams usually reflect what has been going on during the day. Bereavement dreams are common and may even be comforting. Many people tell me that they have had dreams of their loved ones smiling and happy. In some cases, the person who died has even said, "I'm OK." But maybe you suffer from a different kind of dream, a nightmare, or a very disturbing dream in which you wake up in a cold sweat. If the death of your loved one was sudden or violent, you may have very upsetting dreams. Even though you may not want to think about what happened and maybe you don't want to know any details, the unconscious part of your mind may click in when you are sleeping and produce these dreams. Needless to say, these, too, will interrupt your sleep, preventing you from getting a good night's rest. (See topic 76, "Dreams and Nightmares.")

46. I CAN'T EAT

Are you having trouble eating? Food may have lost its taste for you, you may seem to have a lump in your throat that the food can't get around, or you may not have any interest in eating, perhaps not even remembering to eat. Other family members may feel the same way. However, I don't need to tell you how important it is to eat to stay healthy in order to work through your grief.

Keep an eye on your weight so that you don't lose too much. On the other hand, your problem may not be losing weight, but gaining it. Food is usually plentiful after a death, and much of it may not be particularly healthful—foods like lasagna, cold cuts, and cake head the list of popular foods to bring to meals immediately following a death. Try to stay away from the high-fat dishes and look for more healthful foods to nibble. You may think that you don't care, but you will help yourself to feel better now and avoid the weight gain later.

What You Can Do

Try some of the following suggestions:

- If you can't eat three regular meals, try five small ones. Food taken in smaller portions may be easier to handle.
- Have healthful foods around to nibble on—things like fruit and vegetable sticks, for instance. Keep potato chips and other high-fat foods locked up and out of sight.
- Try to take time to sit down at mealtime instead of standing up at the counter or eating on the run. Your food will have a better chance to digest, and you will have a chance to relax a bit, and perhaps even enjoy some casual conversation with your family.
- As friends and neighbors offer to bring in food, give them some suggestions of what your family would like.
- Keep an eye on other family members. If you notice someone not eating or eating too much, you might draw it to his or her attention in a gentle, caring way.

47. I CAN'T REMEMBER ANYTHING

If you are forgetting things these days, walking around in a daze, know that this is not an uncommon reaction. You may forget class assignments, books, meetings or band practice, car keys, lunch, your purse or wallet. You may lock your car and then notice the keys still in the ignition. You may arrive at basketball practice and find you brought the wrong shoes. You may spend hours looking for something that you just had in your hand. Disturbing, isn't it?

I am happy to say that forgetfulness is just another symptom of grief and that it's temporary. When things settle down a bit, your memory will return to its normal level of functioning and you will be able to laugh at some of this absentmindedness.

What You Can Do

First of all, have patience with yourself and your family. Being preoccupied with what has happened, you may find it hard to focus on much else right now. Thoughts of your loved one can creep into your mind at the most inconvenient times—say, when you're in the middle of a big exam. This sort of thing will pass, but in the meantime, here are some ideas that might help:

- Write things down. Don't depend on your memory right now. Pick up a little notebook, and keep it handy. Slips of paper will only get lost or forgotten, creating new frustrations. Organization and handwritten schedules will help.
- Ask a friend to give you a quick call to remind you of important things, such as homework assignments or other special projects.
- Create a checklist to review before leaving the house in the morning. Put your books, backpacks, and other essential items in the same place every day so that you will know where to find them.

48. I CAN'T CONCENTRATE

You should not be surprised if you are having a hard time staying focused on anything. Many people after losing loved ones even find it hard to watch their favorite TV shows. Their minds wander in the middle of conversation with friends. Their teachers sometimes accuse them of daydreaming in class.

Does any of that sound familiar? If it does, then you are probably having difficulty understanding class assignments and studying for exams. It's not the end of the world, but you obviously want to do what you can to keep your schoolwork from getting out of hand.

What You Can Do

- Avoid taking on extra assignments, particularly extracurricular ones, and focus instead on getting done what is required.
- Allow more time to do your homework, as it is going to take longer to do. Put yourself on a schedule. Think about getting up early in the morning to study. Make a commitment to stick to your schedule, and then make sure to turn in your homework! Just keeping up with homework will make you feel better and help prepare you for any quizzes or tests that come along. (See topic 63, "Your Homework.")
- Consider changing your study habits. Perhaps your old way of studying is not working for you now. You may read a page and not have the foggiest idea of what you've read. So, if you own the book, try underlining or highlighting important passages. Taking notes might be helpful as you read. Reading out loud, instead of silently, may be the ticket. Try different things to see what works best for you.
- Have a frank talk with your teachers to discuss your problem and to see what they can suggest. Keep the lines of communica-

tion open with your teachers—they are there to help, but they need input.

- Here's one that can be fun! Build your concentration by playing board games requiring thoughtful moves. You will not only have fun, but you will be sharpening up your ability to concentrate. Even puzzles can help you in this regard.

49. CLOSE CALLS WHILE DRIVING

Grieving can be bad for your health! Because absentmindedness can cause you to have an accident, be very careful in any task requiring your steady attention—using a scissors, a lawn mower, or an electric mixer. This rule applies especially when driving a car or truck. Driving often puts a person in a hypnotic state under the best of circumstances; add some grief symptoms like difficulty in concentrating, blurred vision from crying, and the like, and an accident could easily happen. Dozens and dozens of people have told me that they have gone through red lights or rear-ended cars in front of them while distracted by grief. Don't let that happen to you—you have enough stress in your life already.

What You Can Do

- While driving, avoid anything on the radio that is distracting and don't surf around among stations. Listening to a tape or a CD puts you more in control.
- Avoid using a cell phone.
- Avoid eating.
- Keep a window open with fresh air blowing in your face.
- If you are driving a long way, break your trip up into a series of short ones by periodically stopping for coffee or a snack.
- Pull over if you start daydreaming or crying.

50. RESPONSES TO EXPECTED VERSUS SUDDEN DEATH

To understand your grief a little bit better, spend a few minutes thinking about the difference between an expected death, a sudden death, or a sudden, violent death. All death is difficult, and it takes a long time to heal from the pain. Yet while I do not want to play down the importance of any death situation, in a sudden or a sudden and violent death there are extra issues with which you will have to cope.

When a loved one has been ill for a long time and the doctors are telling you that there isn't much they can do, you begin to prepare yourself for the likelihood that your loved one will die. You are already grieving, and you have time to anticipate what life will be like without that person. You may even start thinking about what you would want in a funeral or memorial service. Most important, you will have a chance to say good-bye. (See topic 15.)

On the other hand, when death is sudden, you have no opportunity to do any of these things. You have the immense task of trying to comprehend what has happened, and you and your family will have important tasks to do and major decisions to make all at once—notifying friends and relatives, funeral arrangements, organ donation, finding places for out of town folks to stay, to name just a few. Most important, you will not have had a chance to say good-bye. Nor will you have had a chance to say "I'm sorry," if there was something hanging over your relationship. You will have been totally cut off with unfinished business dangling, left distraught, confused, and feeling helpless because you have had no chance for closure.

When death is not only sudden, but violent as well, you will have to cope with even more issues. You will need to come to grip with the horror of what happened, what it must have been like in those last few moments of life. Sometimes the horror of what happened is too much to bear, and you can't allow yourself to think about it for even a minute. Sometimes it comes out in the form of flashes or in nightmares. If your loved one was murdered, your family has the added burden of an investigation. Has someone been arrested? Concerns may arise about your personal safety and what to do about it. You might have to deal with the media, the natural curiosity of neighbors and classmates, and, later on, the court system. (See topic 73, "Dealing with the Press," and topic 84, "Dealing with Murder.")

What You Can Do

Every death brings with it a certain set of circumstances to deal with. Some of the following may be helpful to you now:

- In spite of all the commotion around you, look for a way to say good-bye and take care of unfinished business between you and your loved one. For example, you can use the funeral or memorial service as an opportunity to say good-bye or to express your love. (See topic 30, "Why Do We Have Funerals?"; topic 31, "But What If It Hurts Too Much?"; topic 32, "Helping Yourself by Getting Involved"; topic 33, "The Viewing, Visitation, or Wake"; topic 34, "Sitting Shiva"; and topic 35, "Memorial Services.")
- If you want to know more precisely what happened, find people you can talk to who may know.
- If you are having unpleasant visions or nightmares, find people you can talk to about them. Just talking will help ease the pressure. (See topic 45, "What About Dreams?")
- Never hesitate to find a counselor who has the training to help guide you through difficult times. Because family members might get upset, it is sometimes easier to talk to a stranger than it is to your own family.

51. YOUR RELATIONSHIP WILL AFFECT YOUR GRIEF

Grief varies. If life's events go accordingly to plan, the old die first. If one of your grandparents has died, you may feel very sad, but not as shaken up as you would be if the person who died was your mom or dad. You might even feel a bit guilty about your lack of feeling. If this is the case, put it out of your mind. You are not being insensitive; it is normal that you not feel so intensely about the death of someone who might be "expected" to die, or someone who is not that close to you. Grandparents are a generation away from you, and, because we are all mortal, it is to be expected that they will die while you are still relatively young. You may be genuinely sad, but your life will continue on as always. This could change drastically, however, if this grandparent were the person who raised you. Then it would be more like a parent dying, and that would have a wholly different meaning for you. I am a grandparent, and when I die, my granddaughter who lives nearby will probably miss me terribly. This is because we spend a lot of time together. My grandchildren who live thousands of miles away will probably be less affected by my death.

When a parent dies, a child's world is shattered. It is heartbreaking to see a small child robbed of a mother or father, but I sometimes feel that the teenagers are the most vulnerable of all. This may be because this is often a time of conflict between parent and child, and there may be many issues unresolved when death occurs. It is also a time when a son or daughter will be more keenly aware of what he or she is losing: you may be shattered by the realization that your father won't be walking you down the aisle on your wedding day or that your mom won't be able to help you shop for your prom dress, or that your parents will never see your children. We want to believe that there is a natural order that governs our lives and that parents don't die before their children have achieved adulthood. If only that were true.

When a brother or sister dies, you have to realize that it could have been you. And that is scary. More so than other deaths, it's an early wake-up call to your own mortality. Then there is the matter of sibling rivalry. Were there times when you hated your brother or when you were especially mean to your sister? If one of your siblings has died, how do you feel about all of that now? The guilt may be overwhelming. (See topic 55, "Guilt and Regrets.")

Finally, there are relationships outside the family that can have a profound effect on your grief. When young friends die, their deaths are often sudden and violent, sometimes by their own hands. Whether through illness, accident, or deliberate intent, the death of a friend can be a very disturbing event in a life previously insulated from such harsh realities. For many of the teenagers I work with, a friend's suicide has been their first introduction to death. Without exception, these deaths have been very difficult for them to accept. One cannot but wonder what would prompt these young people to terminate all their dreams. (See topic 82, "Dealing with Suicide.")

If you have had a close friend die, perhaps by suicide, you have every right to be shaken by it and to want to express your grief. Just because this friend was not a member of your immediate family does not mean that you cannot take the death as a great personal loss. Perhaps this was someone you were dating and loved very dearly; maybe it was a close friend. It may even have been a relationship that your parents didn't understand or appreciate. What do you do? Perhaps you have other friends who knew how close you were and with whom you can share your memories. They might even help you explain to your parents why you want to do something special to mourn your loss, such as planning a special memorial service at your church or school.

You can feel grief even when someone you don't personally know dies. This happens when someone you idolize or greatly admire falls victim of an accident or an assassination. Millions mourned when Princess Diana was killed in that terrible car accident in Paris. A generation earlier, the world was shaken by the deaths of President John F. Kennedy, Robert Kennedy, and the Rev. Dr. Martin Luther

King, Jr. Who is to say that the feelings that people had were not grief? The reactions of a man I know to President Kennedy's death were typical: years later, he told me that at the time he couldn't stand to think about it—or *not* think about it. All those feelings were indeed grief—a different order of grief, perhaps, from what you experienced when a friend or family member died, but grief just the same. (See topic 74, "The Death of Someone Famous.")

Finally, we must not forget the grief that we feel on the death of a beloved pet. Pets give you unconditional love, they are always happy to see you and sad when you go, and they often provide one's first introduction to the finality and pain of death. If you have had a pet die or lost a pet some other way, you need not be embarrassed about feeling sad. This is grief, too. If your pet has died, you may even want to have a small burial ceremony. That's fine—you need to mark the passing of all of those dear to you.

What You Can Do

The message of this chapter is that grief comes in many forms. It is different for everyone and for different reasons. It is not to be expected that everyone will feel the same way about the same loss. What is exceedingly painful for you may be less so for others. The death of a distant relative may mean little to you, but a great deal to your parents. So what do you do? Here are some suggestions:

- Think about these differences as you react to others' grief. Avoid judging others by standards that you wouldn't want applied to yourself.
- Look for ways to comfort others in their grief.
- Think of ways through which you can let others know how you truly feel about someone's death, and look for ways to express your grief consistent with the way you feel.

Chapter 5

UNDERSTANDING YOUR FEELINGS

If you are trying to hang on when your world seems to be slipping away, I'll bet there are times when you want to shout, "Wait a minute—one thing at a time!" Wouldn't it be wonderful if we had that much control? What you're finding out, I suspect, is that life throws things at you helter-skelter and leaves you to react as best you can. It is to be expected that all sorts of conflicting feelings are going to be fighting inside you.

Feelings sometimes come in bunches. You can be feeling terribly sad because your dad died, but at the same time, be angry too because some plans you made have gone awry, and happy because that certain someone smiled at you.

As the reality of what has happened begins to hit you, a flood of feelings may overwhelm you, making it difficult or even impossible to sort them all out. This is the emotional part of grief, the painful part, and there is no escaping it. But you can help yourself by identifying some of these feelings as they come along and having an idea of how to deal with them.

52. SHOCK AND DISBELIEF

When a loved one dies, there is a period of shock and disbelief. It is always hard to grasp the finality of major changes in one's life. In your head, you know that she is gone and will never return, but in your heart you wait for her to come home. Intellectually, you have heard the news, but emotionally, it doesn't seem real. It takes time for these two forces to come together. You may find yourself thinking, "This is not happening; there must be some mistake," or "My sister has not died! I can't believe this!" It is this blanket of numbness that helps you and your family get through the funeral and those first few weeks or longer. The more sudden the death, the longer this protective shell is likely to last.

While attending the funeral, you may overhear comments from friends or relatives saying, "Look at how well the family is holding up." Indeed, you may be "holding up" because you are not yet in touch with what has happened. You may observe family members laughing, joking, and acting as if the funeral were a party. Chances are, it's because everyone is in a state of shock. The shock and numbness will last differing lengths of time for different people and different circumstances. If your loved one was sick and death was anticipated, the numbness may last for a couple of weeks. On the other hand, if the death was unexpected or violent, the shock and numbness could last for months. When the reality of what has happened is too great for us to absorb, our bodies and minds tend to go into a protective mode, keeping the reality of what has happened at a distance. However, even if this happens, it will eventually wear off and reality will begin to sink in. When it does, it is likely to be accompanied by a lot of powerful emotions. Don't be surprised if you find yourself going back and forth between shock and reality for a while. The reality will eventually take over.

What You Can Do

The more you talk about the death, the more real it will become. And it needs to become real before you can go on with the mourning process. Grief is painful, but you needn't do it alone. Your family, friends, or perhaps a counselor can help you through this difficult time. Talking helps, so don't shy away from it. Cry if you need to; it too will help. Write out your thoughts and share them with others— at least one other special person.

You may be someone who needs to know the details of what happened or who needs to go to the site where it happened. Or you may be someone for whom just knowing that your loved one is dead is enough. Both ways of dealing with death are OK. Trust yourself to be the best judge of what works for you. If you want to know everything that occurred, let your family know and perhaps they can help you get the information that you need. At the same time, don't be surprised if certain members of your family want no part of the details and even try to discourage you from seeking them. It could be their attempt to protect you from more pain. If the death was violent, go slowly as you begin to learn more precisely what happened. Remember, you can stop this quest any time you want to. Because details relating to a violent death can be brutal, make sure that you have someone with you and make sure that you process this information with someone. (See topic 27, "Do You Want to Know the Details?")

More commonly, the facts concerning a death are not frightening, but there is still a need to know. One teen I know, whose mother died suddenly in a hospital, needed to visit the room in which her mother died. She wanted to see the bed, the view from the window, and talk with those who cared for her mother on that last day. Having done this, she felt more at peace with her mother's death.

53. DENIAL: I WON'T ACCEPT THIS

It may be hitting you now, like bolts of lightning, that your loved one is dead, never to return, gone from you forever. The pain of this realization can be unbearable, the feelings it generates intense. You may even doubt that you can survive this much pain. You may be looking for ways to escape it. You may be looking for a Band-Aid to take the pain away.

Sometimes, in an effort to avoid the pain, people make a deliberate decision not to acknowledge what has happened and to deny that the person has died. You might find yourself doing this in one of several ways: refusing to talk about the deceased, leaving the room if anyone else brings up his name, keeping too busy or burying yourself in schoolwork to avoid thinking about it, using drugs or alcohol to numb yourself so you can't feel the pain, avoiding coming home (where you would have to confront your loved one's absence), or refusing to attend the funeral or visit the grave. You may insist on speaking of the deceased in the present tense and become upset if anyone challenges you. You may not want to talk about the death and may even leave the room if the person's name is brought up. You may be pretending that she is on a business trip and will be back in a week or so. I live in a part of our country where many families are in the military and where teens have told me that the way they coped with the death of their fathers was to pretend that their dads were on tour and would be gone for a few months. Listening to them, it is often hard to determine when or if denial—a conscious decision not to accept some part of reality—is becoming a problem. If you recognize any of this in yourself, you may want to see if your denial is becoming a problem. Ask yourself the following questions:

- Is your denial causing problems with your family members or your friends?
- Are you isolating yourself from others?
- Is the way that you have chosen to deal with this causing arguments or bad feelings?
- Is your denial interfering with your getting on with your own life?
- Are you using drugs or alcohol to deaden your feelings?

What You Can Do

There may be times when the pain is so great that you need to pretend that your loved one hasn't really died (*really* is the weasel word here). This could be a little game you play with yourself, pretending that she is on a trip visiting friends in another state. Such a tactic could be harmless for a *very short* time. However, if you find yourself having to work very hard to keep up this pretense, getting angry if anyone tries to break into your fantasy, or it is preventing you from getting on with your life or interfering with your relationships, you have gone over the line; you have slipped into denial and need some help.

You can't escape from having to deal with your grief. Suppress it now, and it will come out at a later time, perhaps years from now, and strongly disrupt your life. None of this need happen, but if you persist with denial, you could end up with serious depression, addiction, unstable personal relationships, and problems in school and on the job. I must tell you that I spend a lot of time with adults who are suffering today from unresolved grief going back to their youth. You don't need that. Here are some ideas on ways to fight it:

- Talk about your loss, even though it is painful. Find people you can trust to talk to about what has happened—people who will stick this out with you, who will hear what you have to say and want to know how you are feeling. If it is too painful to talk about the death, talk about that person's life. You might even get out the family photo albums or videos and invite others to look at them with you and to share memories.
- Stay away from drugs and alcohol. They will only make you feel worse, either because they are depressants or because they are stimulants that will ultimately let you down.
- Read as much as you can about grief to better understand your own grief.

- Look for a support group for teens. If there is one in your area, it can help you come to realize that there are other teenagers enduring some of the same pain you are. You can be helped by their caring and love, and, in turn, be of help to some of them. Every time you share your story, it will become more real for you. As I suspect you are coming to understand, it *must* become real before you can resolve your grief.
- Seek counseling for help and guidance. This can be done through your school, your local mental-health center, hospice, or other community organization.

54. ANGER: LIFE STINKS; IT'S NOT FAIR

"Life stinks. It's not fair!" Is that what I hear you saying? Well, knowing all the sad stories that have been related to me, I certainly won't argue with that assessment. But then, who promised that it would be fair? I can't explain why some people have so much more to deal with than others. We all know of people who seem to go through life unscathed, never having to deal with any big issues. Actually, I was one of those people, for a while. The only deaths I had to deal with as a child and teenager were of my grandparents and one beloved pet. For thirty years, life for me was essentially serene—attending school, dating, getting married, having children. I was thirty-five before my husband died. I could, of course, complain because none of my friends' husbands died, but compared to my children I was lucky.

It's not that there aren't reasons to be angry. Here are some people and things that may make you angry:

- The person who died—because he didn't take care of his health as he should have. Perhaps he was overweight and didn't exercise or smoked or took needless chances. Perhaps you begged him to change, and he didn't take your advice.

- The doctors—because they didn't provide the kind of care you felt that your loved one should have had. Perhaps you feel that the doctors made mistakes.
- Friends and relatives—because they won't give you any peace.
- Your family—because your role has changed since this death. You may have more responsibilities now, and you may feel you had too many to start with.
- Your teachers—because they don't understand.
- The clerk in the school office—because she wrote "deceased" after your mom's name while you were standing there.
- God—because he didn't answer your prayers or protect your loved one from harm.
- Well-meaning friends and relatives—because they say dumb things that can rub you the wrong way: "I know how you are feeling; my great aunt died" or "You can always find a new boyfriend" or "It's part of God's plan" or "It must have been her time" or "Put it behind you and get on with your life." I call these comments "well-meaning but vapid" because they are not made to be mean, but in fact aren't the least bit helpful. I also think that they reflect the awkwardness and discomfort that people have dealing with the topic of death.
- Newspaper reporters—because they don't get the story straight.
- People telling you what to do and how you should feel.
- Peers who want to rile you—because they really can. Recently, a teen told me about an incident that happened in the cafeteria. Some guys who were not friends of his started making rude comments about his mother, who had died. His impulse was to beat them up, but instead he found a teacher who praised him for "walking away" and then sat with him at a different table through the rest of lunch. Teens don't always realize the pain they can cause by making off-the-wall comments. When my husband was dying but still spending an hour or two a day at work, I received a phone call asking to speak to "Mrs.

Fitzgerald." I acknowledged that I was she, and the voice went on to say "your husband has died." Needless to say, this upset me greatly. I then heard all kinds of giggling and the person hung up, leaving me feeling scared, relieved, and terribly angry.

Maybe you're just angry and don't even know why, and this anger is falling on the people you most care about. I see many families who are fighting among themselves. It seems that the impulse is to take it out on someone more vulnerable than yourself. In my family, I must confess that I took it out on my oldest daughter, who passed it on to her sister until the family dog caught it in the end. Poor Rusty!

What You Can Do

First of all, it's OK to be angry if life has dealt you an enormous blow. But it isn't OK to take your anger out on others, or even on yourself. All too often we vent our anger on those we love the most. Patience is not an attribute of grief, but that doesn't mean that grief is a license to hurt others. You may be snapping at your family and friends over trivial matters and saying things that you really don't mean. Feelings get hurt, tension mounts, and families fall apart. Anger is destructive and dangerous. It can lead to bizarre, stupid, and idiotic behavior and destructive acts such as driving carelessly, taking needless risks, using drugs and alcohol, and inflicting harm on oneself.

Being angry is not fun. It creates unpleasant situations and is exhausting. But anger not expressed can be internalized and come out as depression. It is important to recognize your angry feelings, identify them, and express them, but in a way that won't cause more hurt or get you into trouble. I want you to learn to express your anger in appropriate ways. Here are some suggestions that might be helpful:

- Learn to identify your anger. How do you know you are feeling mad? What pushes your buttons? Where do you feel it first in your body? Do you tense up? Do you start to cry? The more you know about *your* anger, the more you will control it rather than have it control you.

- List everything that makes you angry. Get in touch with the particulars. Identify what is making you angry. Analyze your list. What angers you most? When this happens, what is your usual response? Do you later regret this? What can you do to control your temper? Intellectualizing your own responses will help you defuse your anger and break it into more manageable bits. It won't seem so powerful, so looming, or so scary.

- Talk, talk, talk. Find someone to talk to whom you trust, someone who will hear you, someone who will not be afraid of your anger and not try to talk you out of it. Talking really is magic: even though you still have the situation to cope with, talking it out will make you feel lighter and more energized to go on. It is comforting to know that there is a person who understands how you are feeling.

- Keep a journal of your feelings. Writing about your anger will help you externalize it and be more objective about it.

- If you are angry with a particular person, write him or her a letter. Say everything you would like that person to know. Leave out nothing. *But don't mail it!* After you have finished your letter, throw darts at it, rip it up, flush it down the toilet (if the paper is not too thick), burn it, or throw it in the trash. You will be getting this baggage out of your system.

- Get a biodegradable helium balloon and write on it everything that makes you angry. As I have discussed in an earlier chapter, this works because it is so visual; you can see it carrying away all that baggage. Goodbye and good riddance! (See topic 26, "No Time to Say Good-bye.")

- Music helps. Choose some music that has special meaning to you, especially when you're in an angry mood. Or, even better, write some songs that help you express your frustration and sadness.

- Tape recorders help, too. Say everything that you need to say, and then play it back to hear yourself being mad. You might even share it with someone. Later, erase it. This is a very safe, very private way to get things off your chest.
- Physical activity is a great tension releaser. If you are feeling angry, go for a run, get out on the bike, or kick a soccer ball around. And, heaven forbid, you might even clean your room.
- Be creative. Paint a picture, write a poem, or sculpt your feelings. Use whatever medium you feel comfortable with. Make your talents work for you.
- Ask for help. Recently, a teen requested a meeting with me and her family to help clear the air and to look at ideas on controlling the bickering. Grief can bring a family closer together—or blow it apart. Don't hesitate to seek help if you see problems developing around you.

55. GUILT AND REGRETS

Being angry with another person or thing is bad enough. But how about being angry with yourself? Guilt has to be one of the toughest feelings that you will ever deal with. It gnaws away at your self-esteem. You feel terrible, in part because the object of your anger is with you twenty-four hours a day! You feel embarrassed and ashamed. You don't like yourself very much. There is a sick feeling in the pit of your stomach. You feel that you don't have a right to ever feel happy again. It's hard to know what to do to find any relief at all. You're even afraid to approach a trusted friend or family member to talk about your feelings of guilt, for fear of what they might say. Will your friend dismiss your guilt feelings by telling you that you shouldn't feel that way, leaving you feeling worse than ever? Will your friend still respect you when he knows what you are really like?

When a loved one dies, I find that everyone feels some guilt or regret over something. It may be big, such as having said some hateful things, or little, such as not hanging up your coat when asked. Here are some of the more common reasons for feeling guilty that teenagers have shared with me over the years. You may recognize yourself in some of them. Teens often feel guilty for:

- Not spending more time with an ailing father before he died
- Not being nicer or just more pleasant
- Having a "big mouth" and saying hateful things
- Not appreciating the person more
- Having a big fight over curfew hours
- Disobeying and lying
- Not insisting more strongly that the person stop smoking
- Hating those hospital visits
- Wanting to spend time with friends instead of helping out at home
- Resenting the extra responsibilities the person's illness brought on
- Not trying harder to get better grades

I have titled this section "guilt and regrets" for a very important reason. If you noticed, some of the reasons listed above involved wishes and not actions. There is a difference. Regrets are wishes. You *wish* that you had tried harder to make Mom stop smoking. You *wish* that you had spent more time at home. You *wish* that you had gone on that last family outing. Regrets are often labeled as guilt, making them a lot more powerful and a lot harder to deal with. Guilt, on the other hand, implies action of some sort. It stems from something that you *did* or something hurtful that you *said*. Lying, for example, would lead to guilt, as would storming out of the house over your parent's protest, or blurting out "I hate you" during a fight. Wishing that you had been more loving or attentive might lead to feelings of regret, but not legitimately to guilt. I would like you to understand the difference.

Thoughts sometimes fall into this guilt category as well. Teens tell me that they feel guilty for thinking certain thoughts, such as "I wish he would hurry up and die" or "I wish I didn't have her for a mother" or "I just wish he would fall into a hole and disappear." I remember visiting my sick and dying parents with a sister who also had come some distance to see them. When we left the house, I breathed a sigh of relief and said, "I am so glad to get out of there," whereupon my sister said, "I am so glad to hear you say that. I thought I was the only one to think that way. I have felt so guilty for thinking that." We do not have control over thoughts; they just pop into our minds at random. You do not have to feel guilty over thoughts. It is what you *do* with those thoughts that make them right or wrong. If you had the thought, "I wish he would hurry up and die" and had gone into his room and told him that, you probably would feel guilty later for pursuing that thought and taking that action. In my sister's case, she had the thought, but in fact returned frequently to see and comfort our dying parents—no occasion for feeling guilty.

What You Can Do

As you start to look at your own feelings of guilt, weed out those that are mere regrets. Give yourself a break. There is no reason to beat yourself up because you wish that you had done something better. No one is perfect, and what you will come to realize is that you can second-guess almost every decision you make in life.

On the other hand, you need to do something about guilt—it won't just go away. You need to acknowledge it, because, if you don't find relief, guilt can become very destructive, undermining your sense of self-worth. Without some relief, you could fall into a pattern of self-destructive behavior, examples of which fill the newspapers every day. Fortunately, there are ways to get relief from this overwhelming, self-defeating feeling.

You are not a bad person because you might have done or said something that caused pain. We all say and do things that we wish we hadn't—and probably will repeat in other circumstances. It is part of human nature, but it is important that we learn from our mistakes. There are things that you can do to get relief from your feelings of guilt.

- Make a list of everything that you feel guilty about or have regrets for. Analyze your list and note which items are guilt and which are regret. This exercise will help you to be more objective and put these things in their proper places. It will break the paralysis you may feel now and give you hope for the future.
- Which items on your list are still stirring up bad feelings for you? Are there some items that you can still do something— perhaps apologize—about? Are there some things on your list that, to your pleasant surprise, have been resolved already?
- Find someone to talk to—someone you can trust and who will hear you. Someone who will not say, "Oh, you shouldn't feel that way." It doesn't help to have someone tell you that, when in fact you do feel that way. This trusted person might be your school counselor, a parent, coach, minister, or a therapist.
- As in the section on anger (topic 54), my balloon trick works here, too. Once again, write everything you feel bad about on a biodegradable balloon, or on a note tied to the balloon, and let it go. Just let all that bad stuff go. You probably have suffered enough already.
- Be careful with hindsight. By hindsight, I mean second-guessing. After the death, you have all the answers to the unanswered questions. Now you have all the pieces to the puzzle. Before the death you didn't know how things would work out. You didn't know when you had that argument that she would go off to work and be killed in an auto accident. If you had known the end result, you most likely would have done things

differently. Really be careful with hindsight; there is no end to it.

- Write a letter to the person who died, saying all of the things that you wish you had said earlier. You might even take it to the cemetery and read it aloud over the grave. If there was a big fight and both of you were somewhat to blame, it might be helpful to ask for forgiveness by striking up a bargain, saying, "I forgive you if you'll forgive me."
- Set down your thoughts and feelings in a journal. Keep it up.
- Write a poem or a song expressing your feelings. Put it to music if you're so inclined.
- Assign a task to the thing that you feel guilty about and decide on a number of times that you are going to perform the task, sort of like penance after confession. Each time you do that task, remind yourself of why you are doing it and also remind yourself that at the end of this task, you are going to let that guilt feeling go. Here are some task ideas:

  - Clean the kitchen four times without being asked.
  - Volunteer to do the laundry for the whole family two times.
  - Take a younger sister to her ballet classes.
  - Baby-sit for free one time.

- Our actions sometimes give us lessons to learn. As you review your guilt or regrets, has there been a lesson to take stock of? Have you learned something that will make your life better? With all the pain that we feel, it is perhaps ironic that guilt can play an important part in making us better people when it's all over. It can for you, too.
- The hard part of getting relief from guilt is learning to forgive yourself, to recognize that you are human and that there will be times when you just blow it and say or do things that you will be ashamed of later. Think about what it is you did, and, while

not denying your guilt, ask yourself if you are not expecting more of yourself than you expect of the rest of the human race. "To err is human," Alexander Pope wrote, "to forgive divine."

- Don't forget the good things that you did. So often when we feel guilty about something, we forget the "good stuff." Take some time to make a list of all the things that you feel good about, and carry it with you. The next time you have a guilt attack, pull it out and read it so you can honestly say, "I really do feel bad about that, but on the other hand, I feel good about these things."

56. DEPRESSION: I AM TOO SAD TO MOVE

When a loved one dies, the sense of loss is enormous. At such a time, it would be unnatural for you not to feel depressed—it's to be expected. This kind of depression is called bereavement depression, and it shows up in anyone who cared for the person who died. It's part of what we call grief. The length of time that it lasts and its severity will differ for each person, ranging from a few hours to a few days, but generally not more than two weeks. Talking about and remembering the person, attending the funeral, mourning the loss of a loved one or friend is usually all that is needed to recover.

More serious is clinical depression, which will last several weeks without a break. If this is happening to you, you may need some therapy with a mental-health professional and possibly medication to help you over the hump. If you have had a bout with serious depression in your past, or have had to take medication for depression, you may be prone to clinical depression. Because grief can be so overpowering, you need to be very careful. If you feel yourself slipping, get help now! It would even be wise to contact your therapist to let him or her know what has happened so that your depression can be monitored. Early prevention will be helpful to ward off a full-blown episode.

The word *depression* is often loosely used. One frequently finds one-self making statements such as "I feel so depressed" or "I know I look depressed" or "My grades are making me depressed." It is a word that we use all the time, and generally it doesn't refer to anything too serious. But the symptoms we are getting at are real enough, and sometimes they *are* serious. For example, I know that when I start withdrawing from friends and family, I might be heading for a "downer." It will help you to monitor your own feelings, insofar as you can, to make sure that what you are experiencing will pass without special help. Here are some common symptoms you should watch for:

- You feel empty inside.
- You don't care about grades or getting your homework done.
- You don't care how you look or what you are wearing.
- You are eating too much, perhaps gaining weight, adding to your depression.
- You are *not* eating, either forgetting to eat or lacking appetite.
- You are canceling dates.
- Your personal hygiene is suffering.
- You cry a lot more and for no apparent reason.
- You spend much time in your room, avoiding friends and family.
- Your choice of music is depressing.
- You have low self-esteem and lack self-confidence.
- You can see no future for yourself.
- You refuse to talk on the phone.
- You are missing school.
- You feel overwhelmed by simple tasks. (I remember a teen who couldn't get it together enough to even iron a blouse.)
- You are not sleeping very well or you are sleeping too much.
- You have abandoned your usual exercise program.
- You can't experience pleasure of any kind. You are devoid of all feelings.
- You want to die.

What You Can Do

As you review the above symptoms, don't be alarmed if you find that you are experiencing one or two of them. But if you have several of these symptoms going on at the same time, and they are lasting for several days or a week, you might be heading toward clinical depression. It would be helpful to you to seek out your school counselor or your parents to share your suspicions with them. The idea of getting help for emotional problems may be new to you; you may think that this is a sign of weakness or mental instability. But the fact is that depression is real, it is painful, and sometimes people need help to come out of it.

There are times when people are feeling so bad that they look for ways to feel better fast. I am talking about the use of drugs and alcohol and about promiscuity. Drugs and alcohol are depressants. They may make you feel better for a short time because you are feeling the high, but this is only temporary and soon will be followed by worse depression. Teenagers have also told me that they have turned to sex to deal with their depression, thinking that the closeness of another human would make the pain go away. When it was over, they were ashamed, embarrassed, and even more depressed.

If you are headed toward a clinical depression, or think you might be, get help with it. But, short of that, here are some practical things that you can do to help you through a bereavement depression:

- Talk about the person who died. Reminisce, tell stories, and invite others to do the same. If you are worried that your friends may be tired of hearing you, let them know how important it is for you to talk. If you are worried that your friends might be burning out, ask them. If they are, seek out others or perhaps your school counselor.
- If you are feeling overwhelmed with what you have to do, put yourself on a schedule. Write out what time you are to get up,

what time you are to be dressed, what time you are to sit down and do your homework, and when you will accomplish other tasks. Make this schedule a manageable one. Know that you are not operating at 100 percent right now and may need more structure. Make this schedule one you can follow, so that at the end of the day you will feel that you have accomplished something, that you succeeded.

- If there are home videos available with footage of the person who died, do some creative work and produce a video depicting the life of your loved one.
- Put together a scrapbook filled with photos, newspaper clippings, and other memorabilia of your loved one's life. Or, on a smaller scale, get one of those picture frames that have little openings for several photos, and fill it with pictures of the person who died.
- Do a collage of your loved one's life by cutting out and pasting together pictures and words from magazines.
- Write a poem or song dedicated to her life.
- Create a painting or a piece of sculpture depicting his life.
- If this is your talent, write a play about that person's life.

If none of this makes you feel better, you probably need professional help. Talk to your counselor or parent(s), call the local mental-health center, or find a support group. There is help out there for you, and it is available just for the asking.

57. I WANT TO DIE, TOO

"I want to die, too." Is that how you're feeling? That's a very scary and lonely place to be. I know, because I remember being there, and I have talked to many people who have too. For the most part, it isn't that you really want to die; it's just that you don't know how you can live. Right? How can you live with all this pain, with your future uncertain, and how can you live without your loved one?

Wanting to die is not uncommon when a loved one has died. It may be hard to believe that you can have a life without that person. Your future has a big, uncertain hole in it. You cannot imagine ever being happy again. You might not even be able to bring yourself to think about the future events—like graduations and weddings—that he or she won't be present for. Life can be pretty scary at times. You may think, "I don't really care, I just wish I could go to bed and not wake up" or "I don't care if I have a car accident and get killed" or "This is just too painful." Thoughts such as these are passive death wishes. You think that you would not mind if something happened to you that would cause your death, something or somebody doing it to you. I was alarmed, but also relieved, when in a bereavement group a woman said, "I just wish someone would put a gun to my head and pull the trigger." That was a very startling statement, of course, but what was important here was that she was not talking about doing it to herself. If you have such thoughts, you're not seriously thinking about taking your own life. In spite of your grief, life still means something to you. After a while, you will be feeling better.

On the other hand, your death wish may be much more serious if any of the following apply to you:

- You are spending a great deal of time each day thinking about dying: how you would do it, where you would do it, and when you would do it.
- You are getting your affairs in order to prepare for your own death. You are giving away your most cherished belongings, cleaning your room for the first time in memory, saying good-bye to close friends, or even planning your funeral.
- You have a history of suicidal behavior: times when you took overdoses of pills, slashed your wrists, drove too fast, or otherwise engaged in dangerous behavior.

- You have a history of clinical depression.
- You are preoccupied with death and moving closer to a plan on how to end your life.

What You Can Do

Feeling that you want to die may not be an isolated feeling—there may be others in your family who feel the same way. It is always good to know that others are as frightened as you are about the future. Also, you may be thinking that the only way that you can see your loved one again is through dying. This is serious business, and you need to do something now. Here are some ideas:

- Tell someone! Sharing your feelings with someone will ease your burden. You will feel better *immediately*. So, find someone to talk to. Don't just decide that this is a passive wish and let it go. Anytime you have a death wish, it is important and scary. I never play down the importance of someone's telling me that he or she has thought about dying. I can't emphasize this enough: *tell someone!* Don't expect people to know just by looking at you; they can't read your mind. You need to tell them how you are feeling. Ask a friend to go with you to your counselor, parent, minister, coach, or mental-health center. But don't tell a friend about your feelings and then swear that person to secrecy. Think of this: If you were to kill yourself and your friend had kept your plans a secret, you would have made your friend a conspirator in your death! Instead, ask your friend to help you get the support you need before it is too late.
- Stay away from drugs and alcohol. These substances will impair your judgment and put you at risk of doing something that you would not want to do if fully rational.
- Think about this: Killing oneself is applying a permanent solution to a temporary pain.

- Go one day at a time. Try not to think too far ahead. The future is always uncertain, but right now it can be overwhelming. Go slow. There will always be some short-range things you have to plan for, but let the long-range plans languish for a while.
- If you are feeling overwhelmed with what you have to do, make a list. Write down the things that must be done first and then note what things can wait until later. This will save you from wasting time on low-priority things and give you time to do those things that are most important to you. You will feel better having accomplished something.
- Think about what your family and friends mean to you and what effect your suicide would have on them. Would you really want to inflict such unending pain on them? Think about how devastating your death would be to them. You might think that no one would miss you, but let me assure you that your death would have a *profound* effect on all of those who care about you. I know this because of the hundreds of suicide survivors I have worked with. In fact, families and friends sometimes become very angry at the person who died because of what his or her death has done to the family. There is hardly anything that can happen to a family that is worse than the suicide of a loved one.
- Know that someday you *will* be happy again, that someday you *will* be glad you are alive, and that someday you *will* look forward to tomorrow.

58. FEARS AND WORRIES:
I HAVE SO MANY CONCERNS

Your life changes when a loved one dies. Things that you took for granted can no longer be taken for granted: after all, in this crazy world (it's always been crazy, of course) there are no guarantees that there will even be a tomorrow. And when a loved one dies, you discover that even the best-laid plans can go asunder. Vacation trips, a new family car, or enrollment at an Ivy League college might have had to be abandoned. You may be finding out that you really don't have a lot of control over your life or the lives of your loved ones. You may be worrying now about the health of every member of your family, and even your own. That little cough your mom has could turn out to be lung cancer. You may be worrying, imagining the worst, whenever another family member is late in arriving home. If you are having worries like this, you are probably feeling uncertain about yourself as well, and this is taking a toll.

What You Can Do

These are normal concerns during an abnormal time. It will take a while to develop new routines and schedules. First, try to identify what your worries and fears are. Once you identify them, it will be easier to work with them.

- You may be feeling really worried when you can't contact your mom and are convinced that she is dead along the side of a road somewhere. Now that you know that this is a concern that you have, see if she will carry a pager or a cell phone so that when you get scared about her well-being, or have a panic attack, you can reach her.
- Perhaps you are worried that you may catch the illness your brother died from. Ask your mom to make an appointment with your doctor for a checkup. Early detection is always helpful when treating any disease. Another idea: Get on the Internet to find information about the symptoms for that disease. Two excellent sites are those of the Mayo Clinic, *http://www.mayohealth.org*, and Johns Hopkins University, *http://www.intelihealth.com*. It is much more frightening not to know than to know.

- If you have a friend who drives carelessly, tell her so and ask her to be more careful.
- The death of a loved one—particularly a sudden death—can shatter one's sense of security, making one nervous and edgy. Find someone with whom you can discuss your worries. The passage of time will help, especially if some months can go by without some other tragic event, but, most important, be aware that other friends and family members are probably sharing some of the same worries and fears. You can help each other by discussing them.

59. PHYSICAL SYMPTOMS

Grief is stressful. Change causes stress—even good and happy changes are often stressful. If you won the Irish Sweepstakes, you would be very excited—and under a lot of stress (welcome, of course, but stress nonetheless). Now, if a loved one has died, almost everything in your life has changed, forcing you to develop new routines, schedules, and roles within your family. This is hard, slow work, and it takes time. As it happens, doctors tell us that stress depresses your immune system, making it much easier to pick up those bugs that go around. Some of the more common complaints are:

- Nausea
- Dizziness
- Fatigue
- Tightness of throat
- Rashes
- Headaches
- Back and neck pains
- Weight gain or loss
- Insomnia

- Fears of contracting the same illness as the person who died
- Fears of having a similar accident
- Recurrences of old disorders, such as asthma, allergies, digestive problems, or a tendency toward catching cold

What You Can Do

Do not take for granted that your physical symptoms are all related to grief—just know that they could be. It is important to let your family doctor know what your family has been through so that he or she can monitor everyone's health. Keep an eye on other family members as well, especially in cases where you know of a history of high blood pressure, heart problems, or other serious illness. In fact, it wouldn't be a bad idea for everybody in the family to talk with your doctor. Periods of intense grief are times when things can, and sometimes do, go wrong.

Chapter 6

ON RESUMING YOUR LIFE

The funeral is over, family and friends have started going home, and now it is time to get back on schedule, time to go back to school. Isn't it annoying that your world has stopped, but the rest of the world continues on, oblivious of your sorrow? For your mom or dad, that means bills have to be paid, groceries bought, jobs returned to. For you, it means, among other things, getting back to school. You may look forward to seeing your friends, getting involved with school activities, and having a somewhat normal schedule. On the other hand, you may find yourself dreading it. You may worry about being behind in your homework or having missed an important test. You might not even be sure if everyone knows what happened. You may dread seeing people for the first time, wondering what they are thinking. You may ask yourself:

- Will I be embarrassed or treated differently because of what happened? ("He's the guy whose sister killed herself.")
- Will my friends still come by the house, knowing that I don't have a mother anymore?
- What if I start to cry when I walk into homeroom?
- What do I do about Dad's Night now that I don't have a dad?
- I'm still in mourning. Can I really go to the prom?

Compared to the other issues that I have talked about in this book, these questions might seem less important, but I know from my sessions with teenagers that they are the kinds of things that do, in fact, trouble them as they prepare to return to school. If you are carrying such worries and concerns, let's start from the beginning—how to make sure that people know what happened.

60. HOW BEST TO ANNOUNCE THE NEWS

Chances are that all your school friends do know what happened. You probably called your closest friends and they came to the funeral to be there for you, offering their love and support. Through your network of friends, people telling people, there is a good possibility that everyone knows. But you can't be sure of that. Since news of the death may not have reached some people, how do you want to handle this?

Let's look at a specific situation. Let's say that your mother died during the summer, out of the country, and the death wasn't reported in the local paper. School is starting soon. Should you just keep it to yourself? Forget that! This is too big a secret, too big of a burden for you to carry. You won't be able to pull it off, and it will catch up with you sooner or later. Anyway, your friends and teachers need to know that you are in mourning in order to help and support you. They will be much more understanding if they know that you are in emotional pain. Your teachers will work with you to help you catch up with homework and other special assignments.

Let's look at another specific situation. Let's say that your brother was killed in an automobile accident, about which there was at least one newspaper story. Can you just assume everybody knows and say nothing to your teachers or friends? No, you can't.

What applies in these special situations applies in yours, too, whatever it may be, because you can't be sure that everyone has gotten the word. There is no point in leaving it to chance.

What You Can Do

Start by telling your friends what has happened, and let them pass on the news. This is the easiest and most painless way. If your friends aren't close by, use the phone, or, better yet, send them e-mail messages. (You can write one message and address it to all of your friends.) Keep them informed on what is going on: funeral arrangements, feelings you are having, and what they can do for you. If you feel your teachers do not know, either tell them yourself or ask a parent to help out. Sometimes just telling your school counselor is all you have to do. Ask him or her to relay the information to all of your teachers. Getting this information out will help pave the way for your reentry into the school world.

61. YOUR FIRST DAY BACK

You may be looking forward to getting back to school—or you may dread it. Your parent or parents may be experiencing the same uneasiness about going back to work. It wouldn't be a bad idea to ask them about how they are going to handle their return. They may have some good ideas for you.

What You Can Do

Here are some suggestions.

- Before you resume classes, make a visit to school to pick up assignments and any special instructions that you may need. Have lunch with your friends.
- Stop in to see your counselor before you go to class. He or she can ease your return and make sure that you get special help should you need it.

- Make sure that you know where your parent or parents are during the day, in case you need to reach them, perhaps to leave school early.
- Spend a minute before each class with your teacher, not just to say hi but also to let him or her know how things are going. Make your teacher a partner in your recovery.

62. YOUR GRADES

You may find during this period of grief that it is harder to concentrate, to retain information, and to get organized enough to complete your homework. So, don't be surprised if your grades drop a bit. I like to think that any teenager reading this book is a good student, but grieving the loss of a loved one makes it hard to keep your mind focused when all you can think of is that your loved one has died. You may daydream; in the middle of a very important and interesting science project, your mind might be a million miles away. Your teacher may call your name and you jump a mile. Feeling embarrassed, your classmates giggling, you mumble an apology. This can be distressing and may make you wonder if there is something wrong with you. If this happens, you're not going crazy; you're grieving. (See topic 47, "I Can't Remember Anything"; and topic 48, "I Can't Concentrate.")

What You Can Do

Dips in academic performance are typical when one is grieving and ordinarily don't last long. If this is happening to you, most likely your grades will pick up again soon. Here are some ideas that should help:

- Keep open communication going with your teachers. Let them know how things are for you, and ask for extra time or special help. Let them know that you are finding it hard to concentrate.

- If you are forgetful, even forgetting what your assignments are, write them down. Don't rely on your memory. Get a small notebook for this purpose. Don't use scraps of paper, as they can get lost. Ask your friends to call you and remind you of important events. People want to help, but you have to let them know what you need.

- You may need to change your study routine. If it is taking longer than before to finish your homework, allow more time to get it done. Consider getting up early to do some of your studying while your mind is fresh and there are fewer distractions.

- If it is hard to retain information, try reading out loud to yourself. (I wouldn't try this in study hall.) You will remember the spoken words as well as the written, and the information will sink in better.

- Read the material quickly for overall content, and then reread it carefully, underlining or highlighting important passages (if you own the book).

- Don't panic. Even Einstein got less than perfect grades.

63. YOUR HOMEWORK

After the death of a loved one, the world seems different. Some things just don't matter as much as they did before. You may even wonder, "Why should I work so hard? In the end, I'm just going to die, too. What's life all about anyway?" The most important thing I can tell you about homework is to *do it* and turn it in. The longer you wait or procrastinate, the more difficult it will be. Keeping up with your homework will show your teacher that you are making an effort, and he or she will appreciate that. And the benefit you get by turning in your homework is twofold: completed homework will keep you abreast of your classmates and will prepare you for exams. Of course, this is easy for me to tell you because I don't have to do the mountain of work that you may be facing. I am aware of how much work teens have in high school and realize that not only will you have a lot of makeup work to do but that you will be getting new assignments as well. I can understand if you are feeling very overwhelmed. Let's look at how you can make that mountain shrink into a manageable hill. Try some of the following:

- Talk with your teachers and have them help you prioritize your assignments. When you have so much to do, it's hard to know where to start, so get the stuff that needs the most immediate attention done first.
- Alternative strategy: Start with the easy stuff if you can get it done and out of the way quickly.
- Organize by sorting out the different assignments. Make a checklist of everything that you need to do, and as you complete a section, check it off. What a good feeling it is to check things off as done!
- Schedule a work time in each day, and stick to your schedule.
- Work for an hour and then give yourself a reward, such as an apple, a few minutes of your favorite CD, a short walk, or a ten-minute call to a friend. Stick to the allotted break time and then get back to work for another hour.
- Ask for help from your teacher or a friend if you don't understand something.
- Plan a study weekend with your parents' permission. Invite your friends to help you catch up and explain difficult assignments. Schedule study time and breaks and stick to your schedule.
- Talk to your parent or parents. They may have some suggestions that will help, and they might even lighten up a bit on your responsibilities at home so that you have more time to devote to studies.

- Talk to your teacher about getting an extension on a deadline should you need it. Show what you have done so that he or she will know that you are working on it. If your teacher is difficult or rigid, try talking to your counselor, who might be able to intercede for you.

Remember, if you can do your regular homework plus a little of the makeup work each day, you will get on top of school faster than you think. For now, you may have to cut down on your social life a bit, but by catching up in your studies, you will pave the way for a return to normal exchanges with your friends.

64. HELPING YOUR FRIENDS HELP YOU

Friends sometimes are more special than family. You are born into a family, but you choose your friends. Friends can offer comfort, pave the way for returning to school, squelch rumors, give hugs, help with homework, and provide all sorts of emotional support at a time when you need it the most.

Friends can be a great source of help, but they may not always know what to do or what to say. For example, there are times when well-meaning friends make hurtful comments. They mean to be helpful, but, not having been in your shoes, can't really know what you are going through. If you have had a boyfriend or girlfriend die, a friend might say, "You'll find someone else before too long." That might be the furthest thing from your mind, and the remark might make you feel hurt and angry. If your father died, a friend might say, "He was kind of difficult to get along with, so you shouldn't feel so bad." This could be painful because, even if your dad was difficult, you might still want him here and alive. Why do people say dumb things like this? I think the reason is that they are uncomfortable with the situation and unsure of what to say. They grope for something that will be helpful and simply stumble along the way. If some friend makes a mistake like this, try a soft reply like, "That's the furthest thing from my mind. I miss him (or her) tremendously."

What You Can Do

You can help your friends help you by giving them some guidance. Here are some suggestions:

- Let your friends know what you need from them. You might want someone your own age to talk to. You might want some advice on a touchy situation. You might want to take a long walk. You might need a hug. You might just want some release from the funereal atmosphere at home. Let them know your needs day to day.
- When friends offer something, accept their help and be grateful. Say those magic words: "Thank you." Perhaps at a later time you may want to do something special for all of them as a way of showing your appreciation, like throwing a pizza party or sending small gifts.
- Have patience with your friends if they say foolish things intended to be helpful. It is most unlikely that they would want to hurt you. Give them the benefit of the doubt.
- Listen to your friends if they see something you don't see, like signs of depression. During a period of intense grief, you often lose any objectivity that you might have once had about your own situation. If one or more friends should suggest that you need a little bit of help, don't dismiss it summarily; they may be right. (In one of my teen groups, there is a girl who persuaded her friend to attend the group, and the two of them come together. Earlier, a girl brought her boyfriend to the group, and they came together.)

65. WHAT HAPPENS WHEN YOU SEE A COUNSELOR?

I have mentioned seeing a counselor or therapist several times in this book, and you may be wondering what counseling or therapy is all about. Do you have to be crazy to go to a counselor? How do you know you need a counselor? Are the things that you talk about with a counselor kept confidential? Is the counselor going to call your parents? What is a counseling session like? What is a mental-health center?

First of all, what is a counselor? I am using the term very broadly here to cover a range of mental-health service providers. At the top of the scale are psychiatrists, who are medical doctors, and psychologists, who have doctoral degrees in psychology. Both are trained to deal with the most serious mental and emotional disorders. Below that level, there are many professionals, such as social workers and licensed counselors, who provide extremely valuable services for people in various kinds of trouble. Many of them work for mental-health centers; others are in private practice.

Not everyone in grief needs counseling. If that were true, the supply couldn't possibly meet the demand. But in my work over more than two decades, I have helped several thousand people resolve problems arising from the death of a loved one. And for every person I have helped, I know that there have been many more who never sought help. Their lives have gone on, but in many cases, they probably have continued to wrestle with troubling issues that could have been settled if they had sought, or would seek, help.

If you are dealing with something—guilt, maybe, or anger—that is taking a toll on you, burning up a lot of energy and stirring up a lot of stress, in all likelihood you are dealing with what I call a *life problem*, not a mental illness. But even life problems require attention, because, if they are not addressed, they become even bigger life problems. Counselors can help people resolve such problems and get on with their lives.

You are growing up in an era very different from mine. When I was growing up on a farm in Minnesota, there was no such thing as a mental-health center in my community. The whole mental-health movement was just beginning, in part to serve soldiers returning from World War II. The first local mental-health centers didn't appear until the 1960s, and grief counseling as a specialty didn't begin until the late seventies. Today, most communities have mental-health centers providing services that people need to help them to adjust to the many problems encountered in modern life.

Counseling sessions are very common these days, as are self-help groups. I have self-help grief groups for teenagers, younger children—even toddlers—widows and widowers, the survivors of suicide victims, the mentally retarded, and prisoners. None of these people are crazy; they are all working out life problems.

Mental-health centers offer help with sliding fees, so no one is ever turned away. They are there to help people with mental illness, of course, but they also focus on preventive counseling—helping people resolve problems before they lead to serious illness. They can also offer free services, such as teen walk-in time, which is for teens who want to discuss any problems they may have. In the mental-health center where I work, the teen bereavement group is free. There are also emergency services for people who desperately need help now. In some mental-health centers, people will even come out to you if you can't get to the center.

How do you know that you need a counselor? As I mentioned, listen to your friends; they might notice something that's not right in your behavior. You might also seek counseling if you feel that you are not getting through your grief, that you are hung up on something and it is preventing you from returning to normal life. Even if there isn't anything big in your way, it never hurts to get some extra help when you are dealing with something as big as the death of a loved one.

Your conversations with a counselor are confidential. However, if you are talking about something that is very serious or life-threatening, such as a strong death wish, your counselor will suggest that the two of you talk about it with your parents. Your counselor is like your personal attorney; he or she is there to watch out for your best interests.

If your counselor feels the need to talk with your parents, he or she will discuss this with you. In only rare circumstances will the counselor call your parents without you knowing. An example might be a time when you pose a danger to yourself or are so depressed that you can't make rational decisions. In such a case, you would probably feel relieved that someone was willing to watch out for you.

The way in which counseling sessions are run may vary, depending on the counselor. When I conduct a session with a teenager, it goes something like this: First, I have some paperwork that needs to be filled out: name, date of birth, Social Security number, address, and phone numbers. I then ask why he or she has come to see me, and we talk about what has happened. As we talk, I look for things that are more difficult than others and offer some suggestions on how to make things easier. I might ask questions such as "How are you sleeping?"; "Are you able to keep up with your schoolwork?"; "What do you miss the most?"; "Have you had any dreams about the person who died?"; "Do you have more work and responsibilities at home?"; "What feelings are the hardest for you to cope with?"; "Are your friends helpful?"; and "Are family and relatives telling you how you should be feeling?" Usually, a session will last fifty minutes. At the end, I ask if he or she wants to come back or possibly attend the next meeting of my teen group.

Mental-health centers are a resource that you probably didn't know you had or would never have considered. They are there to help you. If you're having a hard time with your grief, find out where your nearest mental-health center is and check them out.

66. MANAGING YOUR STRESS

We live in a stressful world. Whether it is more stressful now than in the past I don't know, but I do know that people deal with a lot of stress today. Even happy things sometimes add to one's stress, and unhappy things certainly do. Whatever the event, stress is often a by-product. Positive stresses may include being invited to a party where you may not know anyone or having the lead role in the school play. Negative stresses may include the death of a loved one, a bad grade on a math test, or the divorce of your parents. We can never learn too much about stress. Understanding it and learning how to manage it will not only serve you well during a terminal illness or following the death of a loved one, but in all aspects of life. Stress is your body's reaction to pressures or changes in your life.

If you are feeling stressed, try to identify what there is about the situation that is causing the stress. For example, if your parent has died, what about his or her death is making it so difficult? Do you feel that you now have to take on more responsibility than you can handle? Are you feeling responsible somehow for the death? Are you feeling guilty for something that was said or not said? Do you feel that your plans for college or the future must be abandoned? Are you beset by family problems, peer pressure, or worry about grades?

How do you know that you are getting stressed out? It is important to learn what your symptoms are. For me, it is when I start losing or misplacing things and spending a great deal of time looking for them: my notes for a meeting, the keys to the car, my cell phone. When I start misplacing things or forgetting where I've put them, I know that I have to take care of myself and to slow down. Here are some other symptoms to watch for:

- You might be losing your temper more often than usual and having frequent fights with your family or friends. Your frustration level might be high, even with simple tasks.
- You might have more headaches, colds, or lingering flu symptoms.
- You might have unexplained back pain or an upset stomach.
- You might have trouble sleeping.

- You might feel sad, lonely, or unhappy, experience mood swings, feel isolated and overwhelmed.
- You might find it hard to concentrate, make decisions, or solve problems.

What You Can Do

First, there are a number of things you *don't* want to do when your stress gets out of hand:

- Don't ignore your problems. That won't work. Your problems will be waiting for you when you return.
- Don't drop out of school. Forget it! I have never known a high school dropout who didn't regret it later. High school is a very special phase of life that can't be recaptured once you throw it away. And if your future seems less than bright right now, imagine what it will be without a high school diploma.
- Don't turn to drugs or alcohol. These things may give you a temporary fix, but they can inflict physical harm and make you feel worse and even more stressed.
- Don't turn to sex. You may think, "If I can be really close to someone, I will feel better." That's rationalization to do something you know that you shouldn't. There are reasons for intimacy, and they all have to do with love. Relief from stress is not one of them. Premature sex will simply add stress to your life while leaving your problems unresolved.

Now that we have the *don'ts* out of the way, let's look at the things you *can* do to help with your stress:

- Find someone to talk to. As I said earlier (topic 54), talking is magic! Just sharing your worries with someone who will listen and offer suggestions will help. (Listening and making suggestions is what I do for a living.) You will still have the same problems, but they will feel lighter and more manageable.

- Take responsibility for your actions. If you have done something wrong—like breaking a vase in a fit of anger—own up to it. My lectures to my own kids were a lot less severe when they came to me and admitted something than when I found out on my own.

- Take time occasionally to do something for yourself, such as taking a walk, renting a video, calling a friend, writing in your journal, playing your guitar, making a few baskets, riding your bike, or Rollerblading.

- Try to be more positive in your thinking. Now, this is easy to say, but difficult to do. I try to look at the stress I am feeling and wonder if anything good can come out of it. My dad could do this better than anyone I know. He was a farmer and subject to all of the things that happen to farmers—lack of rain, too much rain, an attack of anthrax on his cattle. When something like that happened, his attitude was, "OK, so this has happened; now what am I going to do about it?" I try to follow his approach, and sometimes it works better than others. It also helps to have an upbeat attitude, but don't go overboard—you have to remain realistic. Keep in mind that laughing is a good tension reliever, and a sense of humor is one of the world's best antidotes for stress.

- If you know that some upcoming event will be stressful, prepare for it the best you can. If it is a deadline for a school project, don't wait till the last minute; get started early. A lot of the stress in life stems from procrastination. Avoid it!

- Learn a method of problem solving. Identify the problem and write it down. Is it one big problem or are there a lot of smaller, secondary problems? What are possible solutions? Find someone to talk to who is not directly involved. That person's approach will be freer because it will lack the emotional investment you have. It is easy to have tunnel vision when you are facing a problem; it helps to have the problem seen by someone outside the tunnel! Once you have settled on a solution, look at the best plan of action and get to work. But have patience, because some problems take time to work out.

- Remember, you don't have to be perfect. (After all, the human race is still evolving.) We learn from the times when we make mistakes or fail at something. Making a mistake is not the end of the world. Sometimes our failures are better teachers than our successes.

- Learn some relaxation techniques, because relaxation really works. I can have a busy day talking with people, giving lectures, answering many phone calls, and feel totally exhausted. If I can find a few minutes to close my door, put my feet up, and relax my body, I feel refreshed and ready to take on the rest of the day. To get yourself started, check out a relaxation tape from the library and practice with it a few times. Soon, you will be able to do it on your own, and very quickly. It's a great way to reduce stress. You might also find it helpful to drown yourself in great music (like the works of Bach), take a course in meditation, try a sound machine, listen to environmental tapes, or take long walks in the park.

- Regardless of what avenue you pursue, keep up with the basic good habits of eating healthfully, getting enough sleep, and keeping up with your exercise routines.

Chapter 7

WHY DOES IT HAVE TO BE SO HARD?

In the last chapter, I wrote about some of the feelings that get stirred up when a loved one dies. In this chapter and the next, I want to look at some situations that cause those feelings to flare up—situations that might prompt you to ask why it has to be so hard. While what you are wrestling with may seem unique to you, the fact is that others have had to deal with the same sorts of things. No matter what it is, in all likelihood others have had to endure similar pain.

67. POSTPONING GRIEF

There are times when a person has to put grief on hold because of other pressing things going on in life. This doesn't mean that the person isn't hurting as much as others, it's just that for the present he or she has to focus on something else. You may be in such a situation. Here are some possibilities:

- You have an SAT exam next week. You will have to put your full energies into studying and focus 100 percent on that. There is no room for thoughts of your loved one.

- Perhaps two members of your family were in a plane crash; one died and one survived but is in critical condition in the hospital. You will need to give your immediate attention to the survivor.
- The death of your loved one has shattered your family's finances, and you are faced with finding a part-time job as quickly as possible.

What You Can Do

Death usually comes at inconvenient times. It is not at all uncommon for people to put their grief up on the shelf for a while. If your father has just died, your mother may have all sorts of decisions to make right now. She may have to get a job, find a cheaper house, and locate a nursery school for your little sister. In one case I know of, a family returned home from the funeral only to find their house had burned down. Did they have to put their grief on hold? You bet they did. If you are finding that you simply have to put off until later any serious thought about what has happened, the best thing you can do for yourself is to accept that this is something that happens to people all of the time.

Here are some things to be aware of:

- You are not being disrespectful if you put your grief on hold. Being a survivor means that you are supposed to survive, and if putting off for a while thinking about your loss is what it takes, so be it.
- You don't have to justify your grief or how you deal with it, but if people question your love for the person who died, you could say that you have had to postpone your real mourning until later.
- Don't be fooled into thinking that you are over your grief because some time has passed. It will return.

68. REMINDERS OF YOUR LOSS

"I can't get away from it. Every room I walk into, every flower vase, every song on the radio reminds me of her." Sound familiar? Things, places, and music can become bridges back to your grief. As time passes, you will find reminders everywhere: beaches vacationed at, articles of clothing, paths through the woods, changes of seasons, certain songs or kinds of music, restaurants, smells, inflections of voice, makes of car. Each person will have his or her own separate memory bridges. Initially, in the first days after a death, these flashes of memory can bring in a lot of pain because they remind you of how great your loss is, but in time they can be very comforting.

There is not a lot you can do regarding these flashes of memories. They come when you least expect them: you turn on the radio and you are hit with a song that held special meaning between you and your loved one; you open up a drawer in your room and there is a necklace that she gave you. A teen told me recently that the memory of his dad, who had coached him in football, was so strong that he was convinced that he saw him walking up and down on the sidelines. It was very disconcerting.

What You Can Do

There is a kind of exercise that we go through when a loved one dies. As we confront each reminder, we tend to say good-bye to it and move a bit further through our grief. But because there are so many reminders, grief is not only difficult, but it also takes a long time to process. Some other thoughts that may help:

- Flashes of memory are normal and part of grief.
- Share some of these incidents with others and hear what they have to say about their own flashbacks.

- Keep a journal of your memories. They will become treasures later on, and you will be happy that they are recorded. Eventually, you may want to share your journal with friends, family, or even children of your own.

69. IS IT OK TO ASK FOR KEEPSAKES?

Keepsakes are objects that remind you of your loved one. They may be photos or personal items that belonged to the person who died, such as articles of clothing, medals won, hobby paraphernalia, tools, jewelry, books, or CDs. They are treasures to keep, to touch, to smell, and to make us feel closer to that person, and it's definitely OK to ask what such treasures you might be able to keep for yourself.

What You Can Do

Here are some things to consider regarding keepsakes:

- It is OK to ask for certain items that once belonged to your loved one, but ask in a nice way. I might suggest you say, "When you are ready to give away Dad's stuff, I would love to have his fishing rod." In this way, you would not be pressuring your mom, but simply letting her know what you want. I saved certain of my husband's things for my children, but I had no idea that it was the old sweatshirt, the collection of caps, and the tools that my kids really wanted.
- Sometimes families make wish lists. They write down what everybody wants and try to be fair to everyone when the time comes to distribute the keepsakes.
- If it is a friend who has died, the parents of your friend may ask you if there is anything you might like to have. When my

daughter Sarah was in high school, a friend committed suicide, an act that is always shattering to family and friends. After the funeral, her friend's mother laid out some things and asked Sarah if she would like to have anything. My daughter accepted a treasured pair of sandals to wear in memory of her friend.

- If it is a friend who has died and his or her parents don't take the first step, it's OK to let them know that you would like a keepsake when they are ready to part with something. Requesting it this way will not put the parents on the spot and, at the same time, protect you from embarrassment if they decline. On the other hand, you may feel uncomfortable if the mother opens up the room and says, "Help yourself." In this case, you might ask her to lay out certain items that they are sure that they want to give away. It is usually safe to ask for a CD or a poster.

70. WHEN DEATH COMES AT A REALLY BAD TIME

Why did she have to die right now? Is that what you're asking yourself? Death often comes at the worst of times, like when people are saying nasty things to one another. The chance to resolve differences can be lost forever.

The two of you—the deceased and yourself—may not have been getting along very well. In fact, you may have just had a big argument. Maybe you were having some problems with your boyfriend, parted in a huff, and, before you could resolve the issue, he died. Or maybe you and your mother had a continuing battle going on over your room, and suddenly she died. You are left with a heart full of sadness and a head filled with mixed feelings. If something like this has happened to you, your grief is going to be tougher to deal with. But, no matter how unfortunate it is that the death came at this time, it need not ruin your life.

What You Can Do

These are tough issues to deal with, but they are not uncommon. In fact, they are remarkably common. I know a man who lost his seven-teen-year-old son in an auto accident many years ago, during a time when there had been a continuing conflict between the son and his parents. This man still feels the pain of that unresolved conflict thirty years later. I know of many people like him who have had to struggle with what you may be struggling with now. Left alone, issues like these can undermine your self-esteem and interfere with your life. They need to be dealt with sooner rather than later. Here are some suggestions:

- Read the segment of this book on guilt. (See topic 55, "Guilt and Regrets.")
- Share some of your feelings with other people. You may find that other family members or friends have had similar concerns.
- The other person being dead doesn't make the things he did or said right. It's OK to still feel resentment, but for your own good and because you loved him, you ought to try to understand why he did or said what he did and then let it go.
- Remind yourself of all the good times that you had together, of all of the love that that person showered on you, and know that this was still there, even if there were temporary differences between you when she died.
- As I suggested earlier, even though your loved one or friend is dead, write him (or her) a letter expressing your sorrow and asking for forgiveness. Or make a trip out to the cemetery and talk to the person who died, explain your feelings, and ask for forgiveness. (See topic 55, "Guilt and Regrets.")
- Recount the whole story in a personal journal and then write an ending to the argument or conflict. This scenario probably would have happened anyway had the death not occurred.

71. WHEN MORE THAN ONE PERSON HAS DIED

Not only do people die at terrible times, but sometimes you have to deal with more than one death. I have known many such cases, like whole families killed in car crashes. If you have had several friends killed in some accident, you may feel so much grief that you don't even know who you are grieving for at any given time. You may feel numb and devastated.

If there are several sets of parents to visit to pay your respects to, what do you say? How can you help? There will be several funerals to attend as well. Do you go to all of them?

What You Can Do

There are no easy answers to cover all circumstances, but here are some suggestions that may help:

- Talk to anyone who will listen about what has happened. Ask questions about the accident, express your feelings. If you're angry at the driver, say so. If you're relieved that you weren't in the car, too, don't feel that you have to deny it. What lessons can be gained from this tragedy? What kind of memorial might be appropriate for your friends? Keep talking.

- When you are grieving multiple deaths, you are faced with possibly attending several funerals. You may or may not want to attend all of them, and thus perhaps restrict yourself to those of your very closest friends. You should not feel guilty about this, as there is nothing obligatory about attending funerals. Maybe you want to be supportive to a friend who was especially close to one of the victims. If you are wrestling with such questions, I suggest that you read the section of this book that talks about funerals and how to make them meaningful. (See chapter 3, "Funerals, Formalities, and Farewells.")

- Visiting the family of a friend is important, not only for the family, but for you as well. If the person who died was important to you, the family would love to hear you say it. You may have certain things you can say about that person that they didn't know, and they will love to learn about them. Basically, what you say to the family is, "I'm so sorry Jill has died. I miss her so much." If words stick in your throat, just give hugs and don't be ashamed to cry. (Take a supply of tissues.) You may want to visit the family by yourself, with your parents, or with a friend. You certainly don't have to visit all of the families involved in an accident. Visit the ones that mean the most to you and to them.

- If visiting families is too painful at the outset, for either of you, it doesn't have to be done right away. You can wait until some time after the funeral, and your visit will be appreciated just as much, if not more.

- Whenever death is sudden, there is unfinished business, and there is no chance to say good-bye. Look for ways to put closure on your unfinished business. You can do this by writing a letter, launching a biodegradable helium balloon, carrying personal messages, or visiting the grave. (See topic 26, "No Time to Say Good-bye.")

72. WHEN YOU CAN'T ATTEND THE FUNERAL

There are times when it is impossible to attend a funeral. It may be in another state, or you may have been injured in the same accident and unable to sit or stand for any length of time. Still, it is so important to have some kind of ritual at the end of a loved one's life—a chance to say good-bye, to get in touch with the reality of what has happened, and to be with others who have the same need. In cases like this, there are still some things that you can do to show your love for the person who died.

What You Can Do

If you are unable to attend the funeral of a loved one, it is time to put your creative juices to work. Start thinking of ways in which you can participate in the funeral or memorial service from long distance. It doesn't have to be anything elaborate—just something that will help you feel that a small part of you is present. Here are some ideas to get you started:

- Request that a favorite song with special meaning to the two of you be played during the service.
- Ask someone to tape or take pictures of the service for you.
- Write or record something that could be read or played at the service.
- Select a poem or write one of your own to be read at the service.
- Ask the hospital chaplain to conduct a prayer service in your room at the time of the funeral. I once spent time with a hospitalized friend while the funeral of a loved one was happening. We did a lot of reminiscing. It was a very special time for both of us.
- Request a small photo or other memento be placed in the casket of your loved one.
- Write a good-bye letter to be placed in the casket. It does not have to be read publicly, but could be in a sealed envelope, a very private moment for just the two of you.
- If you want to send flowers, think of a type of flower or color that has some special meaning for you. When my uncle died, remembering how much he loved his palomino horse, I sent a yellow, white, and gold bouquet representing the colors of the palomino. It made me feel good, even though no one else at the funeral knew the significance of the flowers.
- When you are stronger, you could plan to carry out your own memorial service with a few friends. (See topic 35, "Memorial Services.")

• Think of some sort of memorial to honor your friend. I know of a young man who died while rock climbing. His friends discovered an organization that offered plans and materials to build shelters on mountain trails for hikers. They made plans, set a date, and met to build a shelter on a trail in memory of their friend. They still talk about that day because it had such special meaning for them.

73. DEALING WITH THE PRESS

If death is sudden, violent, or otherwise sensational, there is likely to be news coverage. Television cameras and reporters working on the story may invade the privacy of your grief. From a news standpoint, some of the best pictures are of people in distress, crying or screaming, but no one wants to be the subject of such pictures or have his name in the paper in connection with such an event. It is easy to be critical of the press, but, at the same time, we all expect the media to report things that happen.

What You Can Do

If you and your family are caught up in an event that commands media attention, here are some suggestions on how to deal with the reporters and news directors who contact you:

• You do not have to respond. Answering their questions is strictly up to you. If you want, just keep moving.
• You can respond if you want to by giving them some of the information they are looking for.
• You have the right to say that you have no comment.
• Because of deadline pressures, reporters sometimes get information that is not correct and that can make you angry, as well as add to everyone's grief. If this happens, you may want to call

the newspaper or TV station and give them the correct information. You can also write a letter to the editor of the newspaper and have your say.

- Share the correct information with your family or other bereaved friends.

74. THE DEATH OF SOMEONE FAMOUS

Everybody has idols—famous people with whom we identify. For me, it was President Kennedy, Elvis Presley, and Marilyn Monroe—a political figure, a singer, and a glamorous actress. I thought that these people were wonderful. As a teenager, I had pictures of them taped to my walls. I watched television shows about them; I followed their careers in newspapers and magazines. I collected dozens of Elvis's records. Even though I was an adult when each of these people died, and I no longer had those pictures on my wall, I nevertheless was devastated when the shocking news came. The pain I felt was physical and intense. I felt depressed for days, and so did my friends. For many people throughout the world, the death of Princess Diana was just as devastating.

It is easy to dismiss as trivial the sadness that you feel when someone you greatly admire has died. What you must realize, though, is that this grief comes from the loss of something in yourself: the person who died was part of you, part of what you see in yourself. Others may not see that, but you do. It's all part of the continuing process of shaping your own personality, deciding how you want to look and act, and determining what you want to do in life—your creation of the person others will come to know as you.

What You Can Do

The grief that you feel when someone famous dies is real, and making it worse is that it seems embarrassing to feel the way that you do. Others may not acknowledge your sadness, and, of course, you will not be able to play any part in the funeral. But there are some things that you can do:

- Gather together with friends who feel as you do. If there is television coverage of the funeral, watch it together. Talk about what that person meant to you.
- You and your friends might plan your own private memorial service. (See topic 35, "Memorial Services.")
- You and your friends might want to do some public service in honor of the person who died. You might consider one of the following:

  - Write a letter to the city council suggesting an appropriate memorial, such as renaming a park or street for that person.
  - Write a letter to the newspaper expressing your appreciation for what that person gave the world or suggesting a citywide moment of silence honoring that person's memory.
  - Raise money from your friends to purchase something needed at your school that would be a memorial to the person.
  - Dedicate a day or more of public service in honor of that person's memory, such as visiting residents at a nursing home or helping some charitable cause that he (or she) had been active in.

75. HOLIDAYS, BIRTHDAYS, AND ANNIVERSARIES

Our calendar year is full of religious and secular holidays. In addition, there are birthdays, anniversaries, and, finally, the anniversary of the death of your loved one.

There might be another anniversary of sorts that will not be on your family's calendar, a special day that marks an important event known only to you and the person who died. If your boyfriend died, it might be the day that you met, the day that you had your first date, or the day that you first kissed. Another example might be the day that your dad surprised you with that secondhand car you wanted so badly. If your father has now died, you might feel very sad on the anniversary of that event. I call these VPAs, or very personal anniversaries, marking events that others are not expected to remember, but you certainly do.

What You Can Do

Some holidays and anniversaries, both public and private, may have little meaning for you and pose no problems. Others may have profound meaning and renew the pain of your loss. Here are some thoughts on preparing for such a holiday:

- Acknowledge the day. Don't try to ignore it in the hope that it will go away, as by doing that you will set yourself up to be miserable. Most holidays have become very commercial, and you can't escape them anyway.
- If that first Christmas is going to be especially painful, have a family meeting to talk about the event. Possibly, the family might decide to celebrate the holiday someplace other than at home; to take a winter vacation, maybe. The change of scenery and release from old rituals might make the holiday less painful. Others might want the consistency of old customs and rituals. If there isn't agreement on your approach, be prepared to compromise in the interest of the family as a whole.
- If you are approaching a VPA, let your friends and family know. They don't have to observe the anniversary, but, knowing what it means for you, they may be able to give you some support.

- Think of new rituals that will put a given holiday into a new context. Open presents on Christmas Eve instead of Christmas morning. Have dinner out instead of the usual dinner at home. Go to the beach or the mountains. Dedicate your holiday to helping the needy. The next year, you could return to your old rituals or continue with your new traditions, as the family might wish.

- Do some nice things that will keep your loved one included in the holiday, even with the changes. Maybe put a picture of her along with a candle and some decorations in a special place in your living room, and light the candle when you are all together. Maybe decorate a box with seasonal wrapping paper, put a slit in the top of the box, and suggest that visitors fill out cards recounting funny stories about the person who died. Later, open the box and read all of the stories.

76. DREAMS AND NIGHTMARES

After a sudden or violent death, people sometimes have bad dreams and nightmares. Such dreams can be very distressing, especially if they recur night after night. I have had young people tell me that their dreams were so vivid and so disturbing that they dreaded going to bed at night, fearing that the dreams would return.

On the other hand, dreams can be a source of comfort. I have had many teenagers tell me of pleasant dreams that they have had about their loved ones. Dreams are such interesting phenomena: They can seem so real at times, playing tricks on your mind—sometimes you wake up in the course of a dream and briefly wonder if that really happened or if it was just a dream. Some people have vivid dreams in color, in great detail, and can remember them the next day. Others dream and know that they have dreamed, but are unable to recall their dreams. Some people feel that they never dream, though scientists tell us that is most unlikely.

Even if you dream a lot and can remember your dreams, there is no guarantee that you will have any dreams in which your loved one appears. Some people want to dream about the person who died, while others do not. Of course, you don't have very much control over dreams—they are like thoughts that just randomly come into your head. Bereavement dreams can be distressing or comforting. The comforting ones may depict the person who died, smiling and in peace, perhaps saying just what you would want him or her to say. We all hope for dreams like this. They're calming and reassuring, even if they're only dreams.

Once in a while, you may dream that you have a visit from your loved one. I feel lucky because occasionally I get "visits" from my mother, who died a few years ago. Recently, in a dream, there was a knock on my kitchen door. When I opened it, there stood my mother. I was quite happy to see her and excited to show her around my house, which she had never seen. When I woke up, I had a nice warm feeling as I reflected on my mother's "visit."

Another kind of dream might be one in which you are doing something, with friends perhaps, and you sense that your loved one is present but don't actually see her. This, too, can be comforting.

Anxiety dreams, or nightmares, are often a scene in which you are trying to reach your loved one, but no matter how hard you try, you can't get there. You wake up in a cold sweat, sometimes even calling out loud for help. If you have dreams like this, you probably feel off balance all day and have difficulty concentrating on your schoolwork or other things.

Whether you are having bad dreams or pleasant dreams, or just wishing for dreams of your loved one, don't attach too much importance to them. Dreams are subconscious reflections of events of the day and happenings in our lives.

What You Can Do

If you are having bad dreams, there are a number of techniques I have offered young people that have worked, and one or more of them might work for you, too:

- Find someone to share your dreams with—a family member or friend who knew the deceased well. You may find that others have had similar dreams, and this will be comforting, but just talking out your own dreams will help them become less disturbing.
- Keep a dream journal. Taking a few minutes to jot down some of the highlights of your dreams will help you remember them later. By keeping a journal, you will be able to see if there is any pattern to your dreams. Dream journals are very helpful to share with a therapist who may be trying to help you.
- Draw or write about your dream, and then come up with an acceptable but realistic ending. After the murder of a loved one, a teenager was having a dream of an intruder breaking in and shooting her family. After the drawing was done, sure enough, there was the intruder holding a gun on the family, intending to kill them. In this case, I asked, "What can you do to make the intruder the helpless one and not yourself?" The artist decided to make the gun a water gun instead of a real one, so the gun fired sprays of water, not bullets. Her bad dreams ended. Now, you might think this silly, but think about this: The main reason we have recurring anxiety dreams is that we wake up in the middle of them, just at the point of danger. Each night, when it is time to go to bed, we begin to worry about having that nightmare again. The thought is self-fulfilling. Because the thought has been rumbling around in our heads, maybe even on an unconscious level, our minds are predisposed to have the same dream again. By putting some closure on your dream, you will have an ending to focus on, and the power of the dream will be

defused. You will have taken control of your dream, not the dream of you.

- Make yourself a dream catcher. What is it? It is a Native American spider-web design woven on a hoop with feathers hanging below and with a hole in the middle for good dreams to pass through. The web catches the bad ones. You hang it above your bed. I know that these feathery things don't really work, but they're fun and they may give you the feeling that you're on a course to end your nightmares. Try one. If you can't afford to buy one, make your own. For instructions you might go to http://www.kza.qc.ca/kzec/school/history/dcatcher.htm.

- Play some soft, soothing music at night to put your mind on something else. If one selection doesn't do the trick, try another. Just selecting the music gives you something else besides the recurring nightmare to think about.

- Keep a night-light or hall light on to orient you quickly if you wake up in the night after a bad dream.

- Ask a parent or sibling if it would be all right for you to wake that person up if you have a nightmare. It would relieve your anxiety to know that you could get a hug and reassurance if you needed it.

77. TRICKS OF THE MIND

In spite of the great advances of science, the human mind is still a mystery and probably will remain so. It is what makes it possible for us to visualize the vastness of the universe, even though we are tiny creatures on one small planet; it is the key to our survival as a species in a sometimes hostile environment; and it is the source of all our ideas, inventions, works of art, visions, and hallucinations.

Have you ever heard of someone's suddenly smelling the perfume of a dead person, hearing his voice, or being touched on the shoulder by that person? Or perhaps seeing something wispy waft through the room? I remember a teen and his friend were spending some time together in the recreation room when they looked up and "saw" the dead person coming down the steps. This kind of experience can be really frightening, since there will never be an explanation of its cause. While dreams are much more common than these "spiritual experiences," they do happen occasionally.

If you have had such an experience, it may help to know that others have had similar experiences—and that they were not losing their minds. The most plausible explanation for these happenings lies in the subconscious mind, where thoughts of your loved one may stimulate sensory impressions that seem real.

One family told me that after the father died, the upstairs toilet started flushing at odd times. I'm not sure, but I suspect that a plumber could answer that one.

What You Can Do

If you have had an experience like this, sensing the presence of, seeing, or even being touched by your loved one, here are some suggestions:

- Know that these experiences pose no danger to you. People who have died cannot harm you or your family.
- Share your experiences with others you trust, to see if they have had similar experiences.
- Keep a journal to see if there is any pattern to them.
- If this happens at night, try having a night-light on or soft music playing.
- Enjoy them; you have nothing to fear.

Chapter 8

TIGHTENING THE SCREWS

In the last chapter, I wrote about some of the things that can complicate your grief. In this one, I am going to deal with even more serious complications—aspects of the death, its timing, and its aftermath that can tighten the screws on your emotions even more.

Coping with the death of a loved one is never easy, but sometimes it is made almost more than a person can bear. If you are caught up in such a wrenching situation, I want to help you deal with it because, bad as it may be, it need not and must not destroy your life. At the worst, dealing with complications of this kind may lengthen the time it takes you to recover from your grief.

At the end of this chapter, I will tell you about something called post-traumatic stress disorder, or PTSD. If you are wrestling with the sort of thing I discuss in this chapter, you may want to know about PTSD.

78. IF YOU WITNESSED THE DEATH

You dash into the house to greet your grandfather, only to discover that this man you loved is lying in a pool of blood, having taken his own life with a gun. Or you are playing football with your dad when he grabs his chest and collapses from a fatal heart attack. Or you get home from school, open the garage, and find your mother dead from carbon-monoxide poisoning. In all such cases, the grief of loss will be combined with the shock of witnessing death firsthand.

It is true, of course, that someone is witness to every death—not necessarily being present at the moment of death but at least discovering the body after death. No one, including emergency-response workers, policemen, nurses, doctors, and hospice workers, ever gets used to this. It is always hard.

One teenager told me of an episode that haunted him. He was on an outing with his sister and an elderly aunt in the family car when they had an accident. He was knocked unconscious for a time. When he awakened, he saw his aunt taking her last gasp and heard what he described as her "death rattle." He saw his beloved aunt die.

Another teenager told me of watching helplessly as a friend struggled to reach shore after being caught in a riptide. He had been swimming in the same area a few minutes earlier.

Of course, we all know of the terrible tragedies that have happened around the country, like the killing of fifteen students at Columbine High School in Littleton, Colorado. The sight of friends being shot and killed has to be one of the most searing memories that anyone could ever have.

If you have witnessed not only a death, but a violent one to boot, there may be parts of your experience that you don't remember—blank spots. This is to be expected and nothing to be alarmed about. Like the anesthesia that comes with a sharp blow on the head, your brain is blocking some of your pain. An example of this is found in the case of a teenager whose mother jumped to her death from their apartment window. As the girl looked out the window on that warm sunny day, she saw her mother's body on the sidewalk below. Yet afterwards, she didn't remember seeing her mother's body; all she remembered seeing were the beautiful, white butterflies circling over her.

What You Can Do

If you have been shaken by what you saw, smelled, or heard, here are some suggestions that can help you put away those painful images.

- Talk, talk, talk about your experience. Don't suppress it because it is too difficult to think about. Talk about what you saw, what you felt, what you thought, and even what you smelled. Get it out.
- If others were present or arrived within a few minutes, ask them to share what they experienced. To use a military term, debrief each other. It will help to find out what others experienced and how they reacted.
- Write a letter to the person or persons who died, expressing your feelings about what happened and stating how you wish it could have been different.
- Use your talents to alter these images. If you are an artist, draw your way through this. If you write, put your thoughts down in a journal. If you sculpt, or write poetry or music, turn your creative energies into therapeutic tools. Share your works with others and encourage others involved to do the same.
- If you are very disturbed by your experience, you should see a professional who specializes in post-traumatic stress disorder. Ask your parents or school counselor for help in locating such a professional. It could be that the shock of your discovery is serious enough that you would need such help.

79. SURVIVOR GUILT: I SHOULD HAVE DIED INSTEAD

You are in a car with several high school friends when the driver loses control and crashes into a barrier. The car flips over and rolls down an embankment. Three of your friends are killed, including your best friend, two are severely injured, and you emerge with minor cuts and bruises. You are so shaken and so depressed that all you can think is, "Why was I spared? I should have died instead."

Or let's say that several members of your family were killed when the family car was struck by a train, and all you want to do is join them in death.

Feeling that you should be dead instead of the person who died is a common feeling, and there is even a name for it: survivor guilt. Survivor guilt is a very powerful emotion. It occurs to some extent after all deaths, but in cases like this, it is often severe.

There are many situations in which people experience survivor guilt. The most common is experienced by parents and grandparents when a child or grandchild dies. They often tell me, "It should have been me. I have lived a full life. I'm old, my life is over, it should have been me." People may willingly volunteer to change places with a person who has died, but life doesn't work that way. We don't have that choice. The hard part is to pick up the pieces, mourn our loss, and go on.

I don't know why some people die and others live. Sometimes, as in a plane crash, the survivors just happen to be sitting in the right place. A person might have changed seats minutes before the plane went down, and the move saved his life. I know of several people who had to cancel reservations on flights that subsequently went down. I also know of a family who felt really lucky to be able to change their flight plans—only to board a plane that later crashed. I don't know why people in the backseat of a car die while those in the front seat survive. Sometimes life does not make a lot of sense, but the important thing is that you are still alive and that you need a new purpose in life. Nothing—absolutely nothing—would be accomplished by your death. (See topic 57, "I Want to Die, Too"; and topic 82, "Dealing with Suicide.") If your guilt has reached the point where you are actively entertaining ways to bring about your own death, you need help fast.

What You Can Do

- Find someone to talk to. If you are preoccupied with thoughts of your own death, it is essential that you not only discuss this with someone but also that you find a professional who specializes in survivor guilt. If you don't, it will only get worse. Your life and the lives of others, as well, may be in danger.

- If you are carrying a lot of guilt, rereading what I had to say earlier on the subject may be helpful. (See topic 55, "Guilt and Regrets.") You may not be ready to acknowledge it, but there are still roles for you to play in life. If you feel that your guilt is so terrible, what makes you think that dying would rectify your wrong? How about a life of public service? Wouldn't that accomplish more?

- Be careful with the use of drugs and alcohol, even if you have access to them. They may deaden your senses, but they will provide only temporary relief and leave you in worse shape afterward. I know of no situations in which drugs or alcohol help.

- Again, write a letter or launch a biodegradable helium balloon with messages to the person or persons who died, telling them how you feel.

- Visit the grave of someone whose death is troubling you and have a conversation (one-sided, of course) with that person.

- Visit the remaining family or families of those who died. Showing that you care, expressing your sorrow, and offering your condolences may relieve you somewhat of the guilt you are carrying.

80. I CAUSED THE DEATH

I remember a teenager who was driving her car when a woman stepped into her path and was killed. We will never know if this woman was trying to commit suicide or wasn't paying attention, but the young driver was devastated. The police were called to investigate the accident and determined that she was not to blame. No tickets were issued, no charges filed. However, this girl could not forget that she had accidentally killed another human being, nor could she erase the image of that woman suddenly appearing in the path of her car.

A classmate of mine accidentally backed his car over his two-year-old brother, killing him. I'm sure that the sight of his brother's crushed body has remained with him for all of these years. I recently responded to a family in which a teenager was fooling around with the car when a friend jumped on the hood and then slid off, hit his head on the curb, and died. Another teen was playing with a gun that he thought was unloaded when it went off and killed a friend. Two young children were brought to me after they started a house fire while playing with matches, burning their little sister to death. Were these experiences devastating? You bet! If something like this has happened to you, you may feel that your life is over and that your family, friends, and the families of the people who died will never be able to forgive you. Your guilt could be, and probably is, overwhelming. You probably feel like the scum of the earth.

What is an accident? An accident is something that happens that you did not plan on happening. While you must be responsible for your actions, there is a big difference between doing something by accident and doing it intentionally. It is very important for you to accept the difference. A person who causes the death of another intentionally is guilty of murder. A person who causes a death by accident is guilty only of inattention or faulty judgment.

There is another distinction you need to make, and that has to do with degree of responsibility. If you persuaded someone to take a ride with you, and later, through no fault of yours, that person was killed, you may feel that you were responsible in that you persuaded her to go riding in the first place. But that is a far lesser degree of responsibility than you would bear if you had driven recklessly and caused her death. In the first case, we're talking about regret; in the second case, about guilt.

Whether you are in fact responsible for someone's death, or only feel that way, there are things you can do that will help.

What You Can Do

- Write down this definition: "An accident is something that happens that you did not plan on happening." Put it on a card and carry it with you to read and reread as needed.
- Have your parents help you find a therapist to talk to—someone who can guide you through this and be there to support you.
- If there have been charges filed against you, ask your parents to contact a lawyer to advise you. Bad as you feel, you are not a good judge of what is best for you.
- If you are comfortable attending the funeral or funerals of those who died, do so, but have your family with you, if possible. If that is not possible, have one or more friends attend with you. (See topic 33, "The Viewing, Visitation, or Wake"; topic 34, "Sitting Shiva"; and topic 35, "Memorial Services.")
- Ask your parents to help you contact the families of those who died. You need to tell them how sorry you are. (If you have been charged, get some legal advice on how best to do this.)
- Look for ways to get your feelings out. Don't keep them bottled up, as they will turn against you if you do so. Physical activities can help release your tension.
- Is there something that you can do with this tragedy that will help others? I remember a boy in our local high school whose girlfriend was killed in an accident that he caused after having had something to drink. The judge sentenced him to community service, which consisted of going into schools and talking

to students about the dangers of drinking and driving. Feeling that his message was getting across, he even continued his lectures after the time decreed by the judge.

- Try to put some perspective on your guilt. People do make mistakes; the human race is not perfect. And people have to live with their mistakes. If you have made a mistake, it is not the same as doing the same thing deliberately. Remember this: *It is not the same as doing what you did deliberately.* You might have a very hard time forgiving yourself for a deliberate act, but you should not give yourself the same punishment for what was only an accident. Instead, look for things that you can do to make yourself a better person, to make amends in some way, and to make certain that nothing like this happens again.

- Call on your own inner strengths. You may be surprised to find out that you're a lot stronger than you ever thought.

No matter how you feel right now, your life is not over. Nothing that has happened deprives you of the right to resume your education, to have friends, or to live your life. I have known many teenagers who have felt the guilt you feel now and who have rebuilt their lives. You can, too.

81. SECRETS DISCOVERED AFTER A DEATH

We don't always know people as well as we think we do. Depending on when and how we find out something we didn't know before, it can come as a surprise or even a shock. But when you think of it, you probably have some secrets that your parents don't know. I hesitate to suggest what they might be, but chances are, you do have some secrets—things done or not done, things said or not said that were kept to yourself. You may not be surprised to know that others have some things that they haven't shared with you, either.

Usually, these secrets are harmless, but there are times when people's secrets can cause great pain, especially when discovered after the death of a loved one. This often occurs when family members go through personal belongings after a death. For example, this might be discovering divorce papers revealing that your father was married before he married your mother. Not too serious, you might say, until you realize that you had been lied to for all those years, and you now wonder if you have any stepbrothers or -sisters anywhere. Other examples might be discovering that your brother was hooked on drugs or pornography, or that your mother had been having an affair with another man.

Discovering secrets like these can be devastating. Such a discovery takes your grief and turns it into anger or, more than anger, rage. You're left with feelings of rejection, abandonment, and wondering who you can trust. If you learn of the discovery secondhand from another family member, your shock will still be as great. There is no way to prepare yourself for such shocks.

If you have discovered such a secret and have been keeping it to yourself, people may be asking why you are so sullen and angry, adding to your misery.

What You Can Do

There is no escaping the pain of such revelations, but the one thing that you do not want to do is keep them to yourself. Painful as it is, you must tell someone. This is too big to handle by yourself. Start with a trusted adult family member, an aunt or an uncle, or possibly your minister, priest, football coach, or school counselor.

- If the person who died was not one of your parents, don't think that you can protect your parents by withholding your discovery. Your mom or dad and siblings need to know what you have discovered. I know of a mom and her children who made the discovery of some secrets together, and the pain they shared brought them closer than they had ever been before.

• Whatever you have to cope with, remind yourself that your loved one did indeed love you. If he or she didn't love you, he or she would not have gone through the trouble of concealing this secret.

• If you or others in your family are having great difficulty accepting this painful revelation, find a therapist who can help.

• Discharge your anger in some harmless way, like chopping wood, hitting a punching bag, or ripping up old magazines. (See topic 54, "Anger: Life Stinks; It's Not Fair.")

• Write a letter to the person who died, expressing your anger, or write him messages on a biodegradable helium balloon, or confront him at his grave.

• You and your family can decide collectively who else you want to share the secret with. Keeping the information in your immediate family may be possible, and even advisable, but circumstances will vary. I know of one widow who decided to protect her late husband's aging parents from a disturbing secret that she had discovered. However, it was hard for her to hear them talk later about what a wonderful man he had been when she knew of his dark side.

• Try to think about all the positive memories that you have of the person who died, and accept that, in spite of his human frailties, he had qualities that you loved.

82. DEALING WITH SUICIDE

In all my years of work, there have been two kinds of death that have been the most troubling for people to talk about: suicide and AIDS. They will attribute an AIDS death to cancer or some other more-acceptable illness, a suicide death to an accident or heart attack—

anything but the true cause of death. In both cases, it is because the families feel some shame over the way that their loved one died. Let's talk first about suicide, and then we'll get to AIDS.

When a loved one kills herself, how she died becomes its own cause of grief. Not only do you have the grief of losing a loved one, but you have the additional burden of wondering why she did it and what you might have done to prevent it. In almost all cases, survivors are devastated.

I believe that people who kill themselves don't have a clue as to what their deaths will do to their families. They may fantasize that their families will be just fine without them. They may feel that they are so guilty of something or other that the world will be "better off" without them. They may imagine that their suicides will be a way of gaining the love they couldn't get when alive. All nonsense. What they clearly do not recognize is that there is *never* a happy outcome to a suicide. Anger—not love—may be what they get in return.

Suicide complicates what is already an untimely death. How the person died becomes something that preys on the mind, whether it was by means of a gun, rope, poison, or fall. How do you not dwell on these horrors? How do you go about grieving the death when you are thinking how wrong, how unnecessary, and how idiotic it was?

Where the person died is another factor. Was it at home or at a park? Who found her? One can hope that it was the police or someone who was not emotionally attached to her, but if you were the one to discover the body, she will have left you with even more to deal with.

Then the questions start. Was there a note? What did it say? Does it blame the family? Does it give any insight into why? Guilt plays a big part with suicide deaths. When a loved one dies this way, it is hard not to feel that at least part of the cause was something that you did or did not do. (See topic 55, "Guilt and Regrets.")

There is yet another issue that I need to address here, and that is the seeming infectiousness of suicide. You probably have read about communities where there have been multiple suicides. Of course, suicide is not truly infectious, but the intense loyalties and emotions of which we are all capable can help create an environment where such irrational actions take on a semblance of rationality. I say irrational because it is *not* rational to end the only life you will ever have for any cause short of a great one like saving another life. The *Romeo and Juliet* story may seem romantic, but it was a tragedy, after all. Neither of them lived to experience what life had to offer them.

What You Can Do

If you are grieving a loved one who has taken his or her own life, here are some thoughts that can help:

- Don't take the responsibility for someone else's life. She did it to herself. You didn't hold the gun to her head or force the pills down her throat. She did it.
- While you may be obsessed by the "why" question, this eventually will become less important as you begin to deal with the loss of your loved one. If your grief turns to anger at the person who died, find ways of dealing with it. (See topic 54, "Anger: Life Stinks; It's Not Fair.")
- If you have any say in the matter, avoid a "quickie" funeral, which is all too common after suicides. When a loved one dies for any reason, you want to remember that person's life, not how he died. Keep in mind that this is the one and only time you will be able to show your respect for this person and the life you had together. Do it in a way that you will not regret later.
- Look for creative ways to make the most of the funeral. I know of a family that was able to obtain some white doves to be released after the funeral, symbolizing the freeing of the spirit. (See topic 30, "Why Do We Have Funerals?"; topic 31, "But What If It Hurts Too Much?"; topic 32, "Helping Yourself by

Getting Involved"; topic 33, "The Viewing, Visitation, or Wake"; topic 34, "Sitting Shiva"; topic 35, "Memorial Services"; and topic 36, "The Burial Service.")

- It is very important to look for ways to say good-bye and to ask the questions that need to be asked. Writing a letter to be placed in the casket or cremated with the body will be helpful. Having a "conversation" with that person at his grave may enable you to say some things that you feel need saying. (See topic 26, "No Time to Say Good-bye.")

- Go to the library, take home several books on surviving the suicide death of a loved one, and read the one that you feel speaks most to you.

- If you want details on what happened, ask for them. If you don't, let people know that you don't.

- If you and others in your family feel that you don't know how to deal with the burden of the suicide, find a therapist who specializes in grief to help you.

- Support groups are another good source of help. See if there is a suicide-survivor support group in your area. Because suicide is such an isolating death to deal with, it can help to meet with other families who have gone through the same isolating experience. In the adult group I conduct, teens sometimes come with their parents, but I also offer a suicide-survivor group for teenagers whenever there is the need.

- You and your family may be worried that someone else will do "it." Talk about this among yourselves and offer reassurances to each other. Keep your lines of communication open. If you know someone who feels so stricken by this loss that life seems to have lost all of its appeal, listen carefully to what he or she is saying. If you suspect that this person is working on an actual plan for suicide, waste no time in getting that person to therapy. It would be especially hard to forgive yourself for ignoring those signs were they to lead to yet another suicide.

83. MY BROTHER DIED OF AIDS

When a loved one dies of AIDS, you not only have the grief of his death, but you and your family may have particularly difficult feelings about the cause of death. You may face the kind of conflict that often happens in families over the activities that lead to this dread disease: unprotected, perhaps homosexual, sex and the use of unsterilized needles to inject drugs. You may also live in a community where AIDS is considered shameful. These issues combine to make mourning your loss especially hard because they distract you from your true feelings: your pain and grief.

What You Can Do

If you and your family are having to deal with a death by AIDS, you have an extra burden to carry. Here are some thoughts that may help:

- Your brother was still your brother, no matter what. Don't let the judgments of others stop you from mourning his death.
- Know that you are still who you are, and your family is still the same family. Your values remain the same.
- Focus on the good memories. Even if there were things he did that you didn't like, think about all the things he did that you loved and now miss.
- If you don't know all you would like to know about AIDS, information is available from your public health department or the American Red Cross.
- Make it a family decision as to who to tell and what to tell them. The more open you can be, the easier it will be. Secrets often catch up with you.

84. DEALING WITH MURDER

One of the most difficult deaths to cope with is murder. As in a suicide, it is an untimely death that leaves the family shattered, not
knowing what to do.

If your family has gone through a time when your loved one was
missing, her fate uncertain, your ordeal has been made all the
greater. In situations such as this, people tell me that there are two
death dates that they will always remember, the first being when the
person was found missing, and the second when the body was discovered.

It is impossible to prepare yourself for the horrendous ordeal of a
loved one's murder. When it happens, you are going to be angry,
worried, and confused. I have worked with many people who have
had this experience, and without doubt it is one of the worst things
that can happen to a family. If you have come to this book after a
loved one's murder, you have my deepest sympathy and concern.
But, whatever you do, do not take the law into your own hands and
go looking for the killer or, worse yet, pursue revenge in the name of
justice. That could only lead to additional tragedy in your family:
first, the murder, second, your arrest and trial. Give any information
you have to the detective assigned to the case.

If you are in grief over the murder of a loved one, you may have a
number of pressing questions on your mind having to do with the
crime. Let's see what they might be:

- There might be a fear of someone stalking you or breaking into
  your house and murdering someone else. This fear will be even
  more evident if you or another family member is a witness to
  the murder. If your family has these fears, be sure to discuss
  them with the police and ask for protection if the danger is real.
- You might be wondering what it was like for your loved one to
  be murdered. Did she know she was going to die? What was

she thinking about? I have talked with people who had near-fatal encounters who told me they never thought that they were going to die; rather, they became focused on escape. It may be comforting to know that in all likelihood, everything happened so fast that your loved one had no time to think that she would die.

- Was she in pain? Maybe not. If you can remember catching your finger in a closing door or hitting your thumb with a hammer, what did you feel first? A buzzing or numbing. Our bodies have a wonderful defense mechanism, a natural anesthesia that causes a numbness to set in when your body has been attacked. I know a person who was attacked by a wild, knife-wielding person but felt nothing before noticing blood on her body. My daughter burned her hands and looked at them in wonderment before the pain started.

- Then there is the horror of what your loved one went through. You may be visualizing the event, step by step, possibly even in your dreams. (See topic 76, "Dreams and Nightmares.") Families I have met with tell me that they can't help but replay the murder in their minds frame by frame, much like watching a horror movie in slow motion. But that is not likely to be the way it happened. In reality, your loved one's ordeal was probably over in seconds.

- To make this death even harder, your loved one may have been raped before she was killed. If this did happen, or if you think it might have happened, it is another horrible issue to cope with.

- You may be bothered by the thought that you could have saved your loved one if only you had sensed the danger. You may be dwelling on what you were doing at the time that your loved one was abducted or murdered, thinking that you shouldn't have gone to a movie or been having a good time when she needed you. Such thoughts are understandable, but totally without merit—no one can be expected to anticipate such a tragedy.

- You may be waiting for the murderer to be caught and brought to trial. This is bound to be a harrowing, nail-biting time. As I said earlier, don't try to do the detective work yourself. Pass on any information you have to the police.
- You may be wondering whether you want to attend the trial, if there is one. Discuss this with your parents. I do want to warn you that sometimes details come out in a trial that survivors were not prepared to hear. Also, you can't show your emotions in a courtroom; you could be asked to leave. And, keep in mind that while a conviction will be satisfying, it will not end your grief.

What You Can Do

If you are grieving a loved one who has been murdered, you have a lot to deal with. Here are some suggestions that can help:

- Look for a therapist or a support group for the families of murder victims. Read what I say below about post-traumatic stress.
- Talk about what you're going through. Share your anxieties with others in your family. Be open and communicative.
- Feelings are very intense after a murder—shock, anger, guilt, the whole range of feelings can set in. (See chapter 5, "Understanding Your Feelings," for ideas on how to bring them under control.)
- Write a letter to your loved one expressing all of the thoughts you have: your anger at the murderer, your regrets for not doing something to save her from this fate, your sorrow in the senseless termination of her life. Place your letter in the casket.
- Write a letter to the murderer, expressing all of your pent-up anger. Then, tear it up or, as one woman did, nail it to the back fence and beat it with a hammer.
- Read a book on recovering from the trauma of a loved one's murder.

85. WHAT IS POST-TRAUMATIC STRESS DISORDER (PTSD)?

Post-traumatic stress disorder (PTSD) is an emotional and psychological reaction to trauma caused by a painful and shocking experience. For a teenager experiencing such a disorder, the symptoms can be very real and very painful, and, like other forms of trauma, require some attention.

When the death of someone close to you is sudden and violent, the stress it causes in you may show up weeks or even months later. The death could be the result of something as shocking as suicide or murder, but it could just as easily be the result of something much more common, such as a car or plane accident, or a heart attack.

If you suspect that you may be suffering from PTSD, see if you are having any of the following symptoms:

- Recurring recollections of the death that are disrupting your home, school, or leisure time
- Recurring nightmares of the event
- Flashbacks and hallucinations
- Intense anxiety whenever you hear of a similar event
- Avoidance of any feelings or thoughts concerning the death
- Avoidance of any activities or situations that would remind you of the death
- Preoccupation with the death many months after it occurred
- Overidealization of the deceased and of your relationship that continue for too long a time and too intensely
- Lack of recall; blank spots in your memory
- A significant decrease in your interest in normal activities, either at home or at school
- Depression combined with increased feelings of sadness, loneliness, and hopelessness
- Detachment and withdrawal from your friends

- Feelings of "survivor guilt," perhaps combined with self-destructive or self-defeating behavior (see topic 79, "Survivor Guilt: I Should Have Died Instead")
- Inability to experience emotions, to feel happy, or to love anyone
- Avoidance of close relationships out of fear that you will be left alone again
- Being overwhelmed with emotions—feeling tense, angry, scared, and out of control
- Feeling that you have no future, no ability to date, to marry, or to have a career
- Problems with alcohol or drug abuse
- New problems, not previously experienced, in falling or staying asleep, or, conversely, sleeping too much (see topic 44, "I Can't Sleep"; and topic 45, "What About Dreams?")
- Irritability or outbursts of anger directed at your family, friends, or teachers
- Difficulty in concentrating on things that you usually enjoy, such as reading or listening to music
- Being easily startled, jumping at any unusual or loud noise
- Experiencing cold sweats, rapid heartbeat, shortness of breath, or other physical symptoms whenever you are reminded of the death

What You Can Do

Many of these symptoms are normal, and you may not need to be concerned about them. They usually disappear in a few days or a week. However, they can be indicators of more serious trouble for you, particularly if they are lasting several weeks or even a month. If you are experiencing these symptoms, I suggest that you keep a diary of their occurrences and how long they last. If they last more than a week, it is really important for you to share your concerns with your parent or parents, or school counselor so that they can arrange for you to see a therapist who specializes in post-traumatic stress disorder. This therapist may recommend several ways to help you:

- Individual therapy in which you and the therapist will work together on a one-to-one basis.
- Family therapy, where all members of your family will work together with a therapist toward recovery. You would want this if other members of your family were carrying the same kind of trauma.
- Group therapy, where you meet with others who have been traumatized and you can benefit from the experience of others.
- Medication, if your therapist—in this case a psychiatrist—finds that it is indicated. Never try to medicate yourself by the use of alcohol or drugs.

Other things you can do to help yourself are:

- Talk about the experience to anyone who will listen. Every time you go over what happened to you, the less powerful will be its grip on you.
- Learn to relax. Every day, do something, within reason, for yourself. Pamper yourself. Learn to meditate, lose yourself in some music, take walks, visit a peaceful place like a park, church, or library.
- Take care of your physical needs. Eat healthy foods, keep up with your exercise program, and get enough rest.
- Stay involved with your family, friends, and school. Keep on schedule and stick to old routines as well as you can.

If others in your family have been traumatized, the following are some suggestions for you to help them:

- Suggest they read this chapter on PTSD and that they find a therapist. Call your local community mental-health center or ask your school counselor for a referral. Your minister or rabbi could also help you with a referral.
- Listen to their stories, even though you may have heard them many times before. Ask questions to keep the conversation going.
- Be supportive and understanding. Have patience with them as they recover. Recovery takes time. Give hugs if you are comfortable doing so. Physical contact at such a time of isolation contributes to healing.
- Offer to help more around the house. People suffering from trauma have a harder time staying on task, getting organized, and concentrating. Jobs around the house may not get done otherwise.
- Even though you are helping another or others, take time for yourself, too. Helping a person suffering from PTSD is draining. (See topic 66, "Managing Your Stress.")

Chapter 9

WHAT DOES THE FUTURE HOLD FOR ME?

If someone close to you has died, you may feel right now that your future is one big question mark. While the future is always uncertain, life for you after such a loss is bound to be more uncertain than ever. The same is almost certainly true of others in your family, unless the person who died was from outside the family—a close friend, say. For now, I am going to assume that the person who died was a member of your family.

You and your family may be stumbling over one another at the moment, trying to get used to all the changes brought on by the death of your loved one. Routines and schedules may have changed, and, most important, roles in the family may have changed. Just because the person who died is no longer there to take out the garbage doesn't mean that the garbage doesn't get taken out! It may be that the family decision maker—the one who gives permission for things—has changed, too. You may even feel that your personal identity is a little bit shaky—death sometimes seems to change who you are. You used to be a kid who had a complete set of parents, each of whom did certain things for or with you—fixing breakfast, buying clothes, going fishing. Now you may have just one parent and feel as if you're half-orphaned. Or maybe you used to have a sister who was your strongest supporter, and now she's gone and you're the only kid left in the family. What does this mean for your future? "Where do I fit in?" you may wonder. It's an uneasy time, this period of transition while you sort things out, and it probably will take quite a while before you are comfortable with all the new roles, responsibilities, and routines. Let's look at some of the things that may be going through your mind.

86. WHAT IF MY PARENT STARTS DATING?

If your father or mother died, there are bound to be some pretty big changes in your family structure, and they are likely to go beyond who takes out the garbage. They're not likely to happen all at once, but in time they could be substantial, particularly if your surviving parent starts thinking about getting married again. You might not like it, but you ought to be aware that it's a possibility.

If your mother starts dating, this could be frightening and upsetting to you for various reasons. You may be worried about what might happen to your mother. You may feel uncomfortable having some outsider intruding on your family circle. And you may be worried that some "parent-type" is going to start telling you what to do. I can't help you prevent that from happening, but perhaps I can help you deal with it if it happens.

What You Can Do

This can be a difficult time; I am not going to tell you otherwise. On one hand, you might want your mom to have someone in her life; on the other hand, you might wish that she could wait until you were in college or married yourself. You might feel angry, as it may seem that your mom has "forgotten" your dad already. It might be shocking to even think of your parent holding hands with or—God forbid!—kissing another person. My kids expressed their concern almost immediately with the question, "Mom, are you going to get married again?" At that moment, it was the furthest thing from my mind, but several years later I did. (They all love the man I married, but they still miss their dad.) I find that the kids in a family think about this first, even before the parent is ready to consider the possibility. If you are weighing such uncomfortable possibilities, some of the following suggestions may be helpful:

- Have a heart-to-heart talk with your parent expressing your concerns. If it is your dad, painful as it is, ask him to let you know when he is thinking about or accepting a date. It really is better to know in advance what is happening than to have surprises along the way. Let him know how difficult this is for you and why. He will probably do what he needs to do, but will be more considerate of your feelings.

- Think about whether or not you want to meet the person who your parent is dating. I think it is wise not to wait too long, especially if she is dating the same person for a couple of months or so. The longer you wait, the more awkward it will become, easily turning into a power struggle between you and your mom. By delaying, you might also put your parent in the uncomfortable position of having to choose between you and this person. If that happened, you could be very hurt and disappointed if he or she decided to go out rather than stay at home with you. Avoid this if you can. Meeting someone new in your parent's life need not be terribly painful—a few moments of your time to say hello and quickly excuse yourself to resume your normal activities is a perfectly acceptable first encounter.

- Share with your parent the pain you might feel at seeing a guy sit in your dad's chair or a woman in your mom's kitchen. The more your parent knows about the particular areas of concern you have, the more considerate he or she can be.

- The rules of simple courtesy apply here. No matter how you feel, you should be polite to your parent's friend, just as the person should be polite to you and your friends.

87. MAYBE SOME GUY WILL TAKE ADVANTAGE OF MY MOM

My kids were worried that I would be taken advantage of—they saw me as the farm girl transported to the big city, a babe in the woods, inexperienced and vulnerable. There was some truth to that. I hadn't been alone with any man other than their father for sixteen years. In fact, I felt inexperienced, vulnerable, and scared. It was a real breakthrough for all of us when I asked for their advice. Their advice was good, and I appreciated it.

What You Can Do

There are a couple of things you can do in this situation:

- Talk to your parent and express your concerns. He or she surely will appreciate your help in initiating what has to be an uncomfortable subject.
- If you observe something troublesome between your parent and the person he or she is dating, share your observation and offer to help. You may be turned down, but, even if you are, your warning may have some effect.

88. MOM IS GETTING MORE CALLS FOR DATES THAN I AM

If your parent starts dating, there are likely to be many related issues to deal with. I will mention a few of them to help you know that, if you are thinking such thoughts, what you feel is normal.

There may be times, for example, when your parent seems to be getting more phone calls for dates than you are, and this may seem not right at all. You may even find that you are in competition with your mom. I know it's weird, but that's the way it is sometimes. If you and your parent can laugh about it, you will both feel better.

89. I HAVE A CRUSH ON THE GUY WHO MOM IS DATING

This can happen, too, especially if your mom or dad is dating a younger person. It can be very awkward for you—you may feel giggly and tongue-tied, say something really stupid to the date, and end up blushing and embarrassed. If this is happening to you, it will help to talk to a trusted friend or counselor about your feelings. Chances are that he or she will understand how painful and courageous it was of you to share this. In any event, it would be best to keep busy with your own friends and be around less when your parent's date is at the house. This will save you from unnecessary discomfort, and, in time, your interests will focus elsewhere.

90. I FEEL DISLOYAL TO MY MOM

If you happen to like the person who your dad is dating, you might feel disloyal to the mom whose memory you cherish. Let me assure you that under no circumstances would this be letting your mom down or being disloyal. If it was your dad who died, the same is true for the person your mom is dating. As human beings, we have a large capacity to love a lot of people in our lives. It is OK to enjoy being with and talking to the person who is dating your parent. In fact, I would hope you did.

91. MY DAD IS GETTING MARRIED

If your parent does remarry, you could be very excited to be planning the wedding of your parent or you could be feeling rather put off by the whole thing. When I got remarried, the wedding was very small, involving just immediate family and held in our living room. I was very pleased when flowers arrived through arrangements made by my youngest daughter, who was twelve. One of her adult friends who did flower arrangements helped her out, even including a bouquet just for her. Do the best you can. Be as involved as you want to be. Even if it is hard, I suggest that you at least attend. You may be sorry later for not showing your parent your love and support at a very important time.

92. LIVING WITH A STEPPARENT

If your parent remarries, there will be many changes, routines, and lifestyles to get used to: there's hard work ahead. I had the misconception that once I had gotten married and re-created the "family unit," things would go smoothly. Wrong. It takes a long time for people to get used to one another, and each of us proceeds at his or her own pace. Life was certainly not unbearable, but it was uncomfortable at times. Allowing each family member to go slowly, we eventually came to where I had hoped we would. My children love their stepfather and often bypass me to call him directly for advice and counsel. Keep those lines of communication open. Talk about your feelings, your worries, and your concerns. If you need some alone time with your parent, say so. I found that I did that with my kids, and I loved those times. Keep on top of what is stressful and address it immediately.

93. WILL I EVER BE HAPPY AGAIN?

Will you ever be happy again? The answer is yes! And that is what your loved one would want. Happiness will come in bits and pieces until one day you say to yourself, "Hey, I'm happy again." But, as you know, life is a series of ups and downs. Other things will happen that will make you sad, such as breaking up with a boy- or girlfriend or not getting accepted into the college that you really want to attend. However, having found a way to recover from this loss, you will be better able to deal with disappointments of a lesser nature.

94. HOW DO I KNOW THAT I AM GETTING BETTER?

Progress through the grief process is so slow that it is sometimes difficult to know if you are getting anywhere. There are times when you may feel as if you are taking one step forward and then two steps back. It's a common feeling. If a member of your family has died, I would expect all of your family to be experiencing something similar. One person told me that she feels as if she is riding on the pendulum of a giant clock, swinging back and forth through her grief. Meanwhile, the clock ticks away the minutes, the hours and the days. She also said that time itself was really weird for her: in some ways, it was going by so fast that she couldn't believe that it was seven months since her dad's death; in other ways, the time seemed to drag. Fast and slow at the same time—that's what you can expect your recovery to feel like. Also expect that you will keep going back and revisiting your grief occasionally, especially at big events in your life. In time, those visits will be less painful than they were the first time around. (See topic 41, "How Long Is Grief?")

Following are some clues that will help you to see that you are beginning to work through your grief. These ever-so-slight clues can be missed unless you are aware of their importance:

- You are really in touch with the finality of the death: You don't have those moments of thinking she has not really died, hoping that she is on a trip. You no longer burst into the kitchen looking for your dad to be sitting at the table with a cup of coffee.

- You can review both pleasant and unpleasant memories. So often when a loved one dies, people want to talk about and remember only the good stuff, when, in reality, not everyone or everything is perfect. There are things about the deceased you realize that you don't miss at all.

- You can drive somewhere without crying the whole time. It seems that when a person gets in the car and starts driving, it is easy to get into a hypnotic state, start thinking, and then cry. Many people tell me that driving is a time when they really mourn the loss of a loved one.

- You realize that painful comments made by family or friends are made in ignorance. People often don't know what to say after a death, and sometimes say exactly the wrong thing. People who have not experienced what you have really don't have a clue about what you are feeling. Still, they want to be helpful. You're making progress when you come to realize this.

- You can look forward to holidays and birthdays. You and your family have settled back into old rituals and customs or even developed some new ones.

- You can reach out to help someone in a similar situation. It can be very healing when you can turn a tragedy into something useful by being able to help another person.

- The music your loved one listened to is no longer painful for you to hear. When you turn on the radio, "that song" is no longer a bridge back to the pain.

- Some time passes and you have not thought of your loved one. Yes, this is a sign that you are moving on. It means that you are getting on with your life and letting the past be the past. It doesn't mean that you will ever forget your loved one.

• You can enjoy a party, a good joke, or the sunset without feeling guilty.

• Your eating, sleeping, and exercise patterns have returned to what they were before the death. When once again you have a routine or schedule in your daily life, you know that you're making progress.

• You no longer feel tired all of the time.

• You can concentrate on homework, reading a book, or watching a favorite television program.

• You can find something in your life to be thankful for, even something as simple as the beginning of a new day.

• You feel confident again.

• You can accept things as they are and do not keep trying to return things to what they were. You and your family have changed since the death, and you are no longer trying to go back to re-create the past.

• The vacated roles your loved one played in your life are now being filled by others or even yourself. This is happening while, at the same time, you know that some roles will always remain vacated—and that is OK with you.

• You can enjoy experiences in life that are meant to be enjoyed.

• You can acknowledge your new life and even discover personal growth from your grief. You are a better person because of it.

Chapter 10

TEENS AND THEIR SECRETS

Over the years, I have met with hundreds of teenagers who have told me of their anger and guilt, their hurt feelings, and their despair. Without revealing their identities I want to share with you some of the secrets that they have shared with me. If while reading what they said you recognize part of yourself here or there, you may come to understand your own situation better. The first person I will call Megan. She was just thirteen when her mother died of cancer.

95. MEGAN

"I resented her being sick," Megan told me. "There would be Friday-night dances, and if it was my turn to take care of her, I had to miss them. I remember one Friday night taking care of her when she had a seizure and I had to call an ambulance to take her to the hospital. I kept thinking that at age thirteen I shouldn't have to be doing this; this isn't my role.

"I felt so resentful. I carried this resentment throughout most of my high school years. I felt I didn't know what it was like to be just a teenager. I felt I was missing a part of my life. My teen years were very hard because of the anger and bitterness. I didn't feel like other teens; I felt different. I isolated myself by not having friends over, even though I could if I wanted to. I was embarrassed for my friends to see my mom and the changes in her. The medicine bloated her face and she didn't have any hair. She didn't look normal."

Megan was even resentful on the day her mother died. Because of her resentment, she actually delayed the family's trip to the hospital so that she could fix her hair and put on some makeup; they were almost too late. Then she fell asleep, and when she awakened her mother was dead. "I still feel guilty about that one," she told me. "I remember walking down the hall to the waiting room and spending a long time looking out the window at the city below. No one came to talk to me, and even if they had, I probably would have yelled at them. I was so angry."

Angry, yes, and feeling guilty, too. "I carried guilt feelings for years," Megan said, but for a long time, her way of dealing with those feelings was *not* dealing with them. "My way of *not dealing* with it was to bury myself in my artwork," she said. "I would go off and draw and paint for hours at a time. What I realize now is that I was drawing about *it*.

"When I was an art major in college, I realized that all of my art work was about *her*. I was struggling on a very important piece of art and had added a group of yellow roses when my instructor argued with me that they didn't fit. I just started crying, right in front of the whole class, and felt I would never stop. My mother loved yellow roses; they *had* to be in that painting. The dam had burst. *I cried regularly for seven years . . .*

"As a teenager, I did not believe in God. I was angry and hateful toward him. How could a loving God take a parent away? If there was a God, he would have saved her. As far as where she went, I didn't believe in Heaven. I just had this sick picture of her in the ground, and that was all there was to it. I thought about all the changes her body was going through and I thought I was morbid . . .

"Saying good-bye is so important, and everyone needs to look for ways to do it . . . With the help of my counselor, we went to the hospital on my mother's birthday. We spent some time in the chapel saying a few prayers before looking for the room my mother had died in. Unfortunately, the hospital had been renovated and her room was no longer there, but I did find the waiting room where I had gone at the time of her death. I asked my counselor to leave me for a few minutes, and I once again gazed out at the city and remembered that day so many years ago.

"I have some advice for teenagers," Megan continued. "Find someone you can talk to. I now know how the years of not talking have affected my life. I was not ready to talk to an adult or a counselor, but I would have talked to other kids. So, my advice is to seek out a support group with other kids who have something in common. Don't deal with it by using drugs or alcohol. I turned to guys and became very promiscuous. I am embarrassed about it now, but that was my way of searching and looking for help."

96. SCOTT

Scott was sixteen when his older brother, Joe, died in an auto accident just days before his eighteenth birthday. The two had been very close. When one took guitar lessons, he taught the other. They taught each other popular songs and even sang duets. When Joe quit his paper route, Scott took over.

"I was just getting ready to leave the house," Scott recounted, "when I noticed the father of my brother's best friend coming up the walk wearing a very serious, distraught expression. I thought my brother and his friend must have gotten into some kind of trouble, and I waited outside until my parents called me in to tell me that there had been a car accident and that maybe my brother was involved in it. The three of us then went to a funeral home where there was a body waiting to be identified. My parents went inside while I waited outside. I wasn't asked to go inside with them, and I think that was better for me. At least I didn't have to feel obligated to do it. It turned out that the body was my brother Joe's."

In the painful hours and days that followed, many of Scott's friends visited. One was his best friend, Bill, who, Scott said, was a great help to him. Others went too far—especially one boy, the son of family friends, whom he hadn't seen for a long time.

"This guy decided his duty in life was to make sure I did not get upset. He observed every move I made. I couldn't get away from him. I wanted, or needed, some alone time where I could be sad, unhappy, or cry, and he saw to it that I couldn't do that!

"People need to be sensitive about what they say to people when a loved one has died. For example, at the viewing, my dad came out and announced that the casket was going to be closed, but that if anyone needed or wished to see Joe again, now was the time. This same guy responded with, 'Well, I think I want to. I haven't seen him for a long time.' That comment still hurts.

"Another example was the nasty comment of an adult. During the funeral, my younger brother got so upset that he became nauseated and had to leave to vomit in a nearby stairwell. Later, this adult was heard to say, 'He should have better control.'

"Overall, I was impressed with the number of people who attended my brother's funeral, but it was difficult to be sitting up front where everyone was watching us. If I was in control, I felt maybe I shouldn't be, and when I needed to cry, I didn't want people to see me."

Joe's death had a powerful effect on Scott. "My brother was a special sort of a role model for me," he said. "He taught me what to do with my raging hormones, that what was happening in me was not a sickness but natural adolescence. I could observe his attempts at independence—the family rebel. I was scared of him, yet fascinated by him and at times envied him. He was plowing the way to adulthood, and then he disappeared. Suddenly I was alone. My younger siblings were close to each other, but my cohort was gone.

"In the years since, I have become much closer to my other siblings, and I only regret that Joe and I never had a chance to know each other as adults.

"The sad fact is that Joe had some problems and often had open conflicts with my parents. But when he died, he became a saint, an icon that I didn't really recognize or identify with. The bitter, controversial sides of him had disappeared. A huge picture frame with many small pictures of him appeared. If any of the other kids were in any of those pictures, they had been cut out. Only Joe, the saint, remained. Now people only spoke of the good things about him. This did give me some solace, however, knowing that if I died, people would only talk about and remember the good sides of me. I could become at least half a saint.

"Joe often made a statement that he would 'die young and leave a beautiful body.' Do I think he had some premonition of dying? I don't know. But he did lead a dangerous life at times. He liked driving fast, taking chances. Explosives and gunpowder recipes enthralled him. He seemed fascinated with death and danger. Perhaps he was aware that he was living on the edge.

"There came a time that I had outlived him. I was then older than he had been [when he died] and I realized that I would have to become my own role model. I had always known that there would be a time that his job as my role model would end, because we had different personalities. That didn't make the situation any easier. I spent a number of years in confusion, with a strong need to be independent. I had to, and did, find my own way, but the search took me nearly halfway around the world before I could stake out my own realm of adulthood. I don't recommend that as a model for anyone else, but it's what I had to do, and it worked for me."

97. NATALIE

"The horror and pain of suicide are a part of my everyday life," Natalie told me. She was eighteen when we spoke, and it had been three years since her father took his own life.

"The shock when I found out that my father had died was more than I could bear," she stated. "I remember the moment when my mother told me, what I was wearing, what I had just eaten, and what I had done that day. It happened to be my birthday. When she told me, I remember feeling alone and confused. I felt as though I had nowhere to turn . . .

"After a suicide, the people that suffer are the people who were closest to the deceased. The person who killed himself does not feel the pain, but the family members and friends, the survivors of suicide, deal with that pain every day of their lives.

"People do not understand the pain that is inflicted on the survivors of suicide. We need help, too; we are the ones who suffer in the long run.

"I will always wonder why and ask myself if it was me. I will never understand how my father felt or be able to comprehend why he did what he did. This experience has molded me into a different person, and I need a major support system to become a stable person again.

"By a major support system, I mean that I need friends and family around me who will listen. It takes years and years to recover, and through all of those years I need people who are there for me. Some times are worse than others—some days are bad for no particular reason, and some are bad because of a holiday or anniversary or a special day in my life. Happy times for some people become sad times for me. My father never saw me learn to drive, he will never see me graduate, he will never walk me down the aisle, and he will never become a grandfather . . .

"I understand that suicide can make people feel uncomfortable and unsure of how to act or what to say around me. I just want them to be sensitive to what is said in relation to fathers, because I don't have one."

98. CYNTHIA

"I knew that something was wrong—like, not with her, but that something was wrong somewhere," Cynthia told me. "When I found out, I wasn't expecting it, but I wasn't surprised, either. She was never really 'happy.' I mean, she would have moments, but mostly she was depressed. I knew how she felt. I guess I am one of the few she showed her real self to. For everyone else she put on a happy face."

Cynthia was sixteen when her nineteen-year-old sister committed suicide.

"It was Memorial Day weekend, and we were at our beach place on the river," she told me. "I was driving home, and for some reason I just burst into tears. I wondered what was wrong with me. Why am I crying? When I got home, my parents were already home. It was like my mom and I were waiting for something—we were both really restless. We started to play poker, and we don't often play poker. Then I went out with friends. I got paged by my parents, so I called them back and said, 'What's wrong?' It was my dad. He was crying, and my dad doesn't cry. I've only seen him cry three times in my whole life. When I was driving home, I was thinking, 'Please, God, don't let anything happen to my sister or my dog' because I knew that my parents were OK and that only something happening to my sister or my dog would make my parents so hysterical.

"When I got home, I asked them what was going on. They were both crying, and they were standing in the living room. I said, 'What is going on?' Dad said, 'Maria is gone!' I said, 'What are you talking about? Is she dead? What are you talking about? You're lying! You're lying!' I was backing away from them. It was dark in the house, and I bumped up against the wall. After I recovered, I asked 'What happened?' My parents said, 'We don't know.' Mom said that she called Maria's apartment, and a cop answered the phone and told us that they were supposed to send a policeman to our house to tell us, but my mom called before they had a chance to do that. So that is how my mom found out that Maria was dead.

"When I talked to the policeman, I asked him what happened, and he said something like, 'It appears she killed herself.' I asked, 'Is there a note?' And the policeman said, 'I think there is a note, there are Scrabble pieces on the floor and it says, 'MARIA AND ASHES ARE GOING TO HEAVEN.' [Her cat, Ashes, was found a day later, hiding in a closet.]

"I guess my mom and my nanny, my mom's mom, wanted to have an open casket, so I tried to put makeup on my sister but couldn't get it right, so I had to let the lady do it for me. My mom had given me a little angel pin for Christmas a year ago, and we put in her coffin along with this bracelet I had made for her, and my dad put one of his business cards in there also because he was always giving her his business card. He wrote a note on the back of it, and I made a card and put it in the casket, too . . .

"At the funeral, all of those pews were filled. My friends all knew her, and everybody loved her. Not everyone knew *what had happened.* Not everybody knew she had killed herself. I guess my uncle told my mom that it would be better, and they decided to say she had had an aneurysm in her brain because she had had a seizure disorder that just showed up about a year and a half or two years before. She had been in a car accident ten years before and scar tissue had formed, causing the seizures and eventually the aneurysm. That was the story I was supposed to tell my friends.

"How am I supposed to deal with this if I'm lying? It's different when somebody kills themselves. Out of respect for my mom, I only told my close friends. But when I lied, I would get sick to my stomach. Why, why should I have to lie? . . . I think it's really my nanny who doesn't know yet . . .

"Pretty much, if you tell a couple of people, the rest of your friends find out. It's hard if you're in high school, because if you're in school, everybody is going to know. When several of our friends died, it kind of brought us closer together, as we comforted each other. But if it's just you by yourself, and the whole school doesn't know your brother or sister, people can be jerks, really mean . . .

"I was just irritated with everyone. Nobody would do anything right. Some people's reactions would irritate me and I felt like, 'Just go away and leave me alone.' Then I ended up being the one comforting everybody else . . .

"Groups are helpful, and the group I go to helps me a lot. You find people who have gone through the same thing, and you talk about being afraid and why. It just feels better to know that there are other people out there and that you are not alone.

"Writing helps, too. Writing is important to me. Writing, you don't have to let anyone see it. It's amazing how much better I feel after I write."

99. KAREN

"The summer of 1986—I remember it as the heyday of my adolescence," Karen told me. "I was fifteen. I had finally been allowed to lease a horse. The girls who also kept horses at the barn were my best friends. We rode together—often lazy, shaded trail rides in a nearby park, or horse shows on weekends. My mom and dad had begun to loosen their parental grip on me a bit. I was allowed to drive with friends—seat-belted, of course. So, that summer was also marked by the elation of being able to sit in a vehicle manned by one of my peers. This meant endless trips to McDonald's and 7-Eleven. I earned money as a substitute lifeguard at a neighborhood pool. I discovered the Grateful Dead. I argued often and fervently for a later curfew.

"I remember such an argument before I went off with friends on July fourth. And also on July seventh—the night of my first rock concert (the Dead and Bob Dylan at RFK Stadium). On July tenth my dad died.

"His sickness was quick and dirty. It seemed to me that the cancer struck him down within a matter of weeks. In May, a lump had shown up in his forearm. It was written off as a strain of some sort. My dad had just retired from the navy, and he and my mom were preoccupied with enjoying this landmark and focusing on his career change. By June, the doctors had figured out it was cancer in his arm. Mom and Dad began making many trips to the navy hospital in Bethesda. By late June, the cancer in his arm was not going away; rather, it was spreading. My dad began to look sick. His tall, healthy frame had become thin and frail within days. He was losing his hair. My parents were either always at the hospital or on the phone long-distance with some specialist. I remember realizing that my dad was *really* sick. But it never occurred to me he would die. I just assumed that he would get better.

"By July, he could only sit, or move very slowly. I think he was breathing with the help of some sort of equipment. But he still had the energy to argue with me over curfews. This made me feel both guilty and reassured. I tried to stay at the barn as much as possible.

"In July, my dad's entire right arm was amputated. Surely this will get all that cancer, I thought to myself. I made him a get-well card with magazine clippings. I had cut off various body parts of models. Inside, I said something to the effect that it didn't matter what he was missing—he was still a great dad.

"On July eighth, my mom and I were at home when he had a stroke. An ambulance came and he was loaded onto a stretcher and whisked away. He had smiled at me, but because of the stroke, it was only a half smile. I kissed him and said everything would be OK. He told me he loved me. The ambulance did not put the siren on, as if not to alarm us, but the twirling, silent red lights warned of the dire situation. My mom went off to the hospital with him, while I stayed at home. I felt like I had said good-bye, but my brother and sister had not. Dad went into a coma at the hospital, and on the tenth, he died.

"Part of me was in shock and couldn't imagine going on with life, and the other part snapped into oldest-responsible-child mode. I told myself that he was relieved of the awful pain he had been in during the last month, though I inwardly scoffed at anyone who told me this was 'God's plan.' I constantly told family and friends we were lucky that he did not have to endure that sickness for years, the way some cancer patients do. My best friend told me she would have rather had my dad for a short period of time than to have her own father, who was uninvolved and remote, for a lifetime. I carried this thought with me, reminding myself how lucky I was to have experienced such a special father, even if it was for a short time.

"Looking back, I think that I initially went through the proper motions of grief in order to reassure everyone that I was OK. Part of my initial grief was for my mom. I could only imagine how it would be to lose a partner and best friend, and have to then face raising three kids alone. I mourned for my brother and sister, too. My sister, who was only ten, had missed out on the extra years I had with my dad. And my brother, who at fourteen was withdrawn and tearless, seemed to not feel as free to express his feelings openly. And I felt extreme sadness for my dad. I wondered how he felt during his last few hours of consciousness, knowing that he was dying and leaving his family. The thought of this pain he had to endure during the last days of his life broke my heart and angered me.

"But looking back some years later, it became painfully clear that I neglected to grieve for myself, my loss. My God, I breezed through the first three or four years after Dad's death with flying colors. The day after he died, I was back at the barn doing chores and riding. I didn't love high school, but I tolerated it quite well. My friendships grew, I kept up good grades and managed to fit in an activity or two between all my barn time and homework. I even traveled to Russia with an educational group my senior year.

"I moved on to college, and after the first few apprehensive days, it became everything an ideal freshman year should be: full of new friends, parties, crushes, and some studying in between. My lottery-assigned freshman roommate became my best friend, who I would live with throughout all four years of college. I dabbled in various activities—the riding team, crew, and the school paper. I brought friends home on school breaks. I had occasional dates and severe cases of lust. I spent my summers at school, taking classes and waiting tables. I studied in England for a junior semester and traveled around Europe with friends. I returned back to school, looking forward to a final, fun-filled year.

"My senior year didn't quite go as I anticipated. I found that I was extremely unhappy—so much so that I felt I had no choice but to reach out for help. I ended up seeing a therapist twice a week throughout my senior year.

"My depression didn't just appear overnight. In retrospect, I know that by my second year in college, it was there under the surface. I experienced mild bouts of sadness while abroad, which I attributed to homesickness. But by the beginning of my senior year, I couldn't ignore it anymore. I cried often, slept sporadically, had no appetite or ate mindlessly. Making it to classes I should have enjoyed was a struggle—I skipped more often than not. My grades suffered; I was dangerously close to failing my classes. I broke off a relationship with a great guy I had begun dating that summer and had little interest in going out and being social. The friends I confided in tried to reassure me that they felt 'off' too. The prospect of graduation and 'real life' was scary. But I didn't feel scared as much as I felt empty.

"Seeking out help was the best thing I could have done for myself. Right after my dad's death, my mom had insisted that my brother and sister see a counselor. At that time, I felt no need for counseling. . . . I was fine. But six years later, I found I was not fine. My dad's death was not the entire reason I became depressed at this later time, but it was a big factor. I came to understand how I had focused so much on those around me, reassuring my family that I was handling things, giving my mom one less thing to be concerned about. My need to grieve and be sad *for myself* was tucked away, only to come out during a vulnerable time when I was indeed anxious figuring out who I was as an adult.

"It felt good to talk to an objective, uninvolved person about my loss. I learned to appreciate that period of depression, and the periods of sadness I feel to this day, as reminders to tune in to myself. And I've also come to appreciate sadness for the way it can make happiness all the more sweet.

"And now that it has been almost eleven years since dad died, I am at times astounded that I have made it this far. When he first died, I wondered how my family could endure a year, no less eleven. But, on the other hand, I am not so surprised. The cliché is right— time can do wonders for healing. As it passes, it gives you confidence: I've made it through eleven years, so I can make it through eleven more. But, mostly, I just plain miss him. Occasionally someone will say I am like my dad in the way I do something. I like being reminded of this. His life and death have helped make me who I am today."

Chapter 11

WHAT FRIENDS CAN DO

This book was written for people in grief, but throughout the book I also mention the role of friends—people who play a most important role in the life of a teenager. In this chapter, I want to spell out what friends can do to help when tragedy strikes. If you have come to this book for advice in helping a friend who is grieving some terrible loss, you might want to start with this chapter. If you are the friend in need of help, you might share this chapter—even the whole book—with your best friend.

I don't have to tell you, I'm sure, that teens are very tuned in to friends, often more so than to family members. A friend is almost always the first person that a troubled or grieving teen will turn to for comfort, advice, understanding, and support. Teens often feel that only friends can really understand what is going on, and maybe they're right. I can't say enough about how important friends are in times of personal tragedy.

Being a friend in such circumstances puts some responsibility on you. How do you carry it out? If a friend has experienced the death of a loved one, you might find yourself feeling overwhelmed by the experience. Maybe nothing like this has ever happened to you, and you can't imagine what your friend may be going through. Your instincts combined with your knowledge of that person's innermost feelings will help you to know what your friend needs right now. Your impulse may be to go see your friend. That's good. Don't stay away because you think you might be intruding. Your friend needs you and needs the comfort that you can provide. But then what? What do you say? Should you try to cheer your friend up by changing the subject? By suggesting the two of you go to a movie? Or should you talk about what happened? What do you tell other mutual friends? Should you say anything at all? What else can you do? Should you go to the funeral? What are funerals like?

Getting over the death of a loved one takes a long time, and your friend is going to need your love and support for a long time. Here are some suggestions for getting started:

- Read the parts of this book that pertain to your friend's situation. (See the table of contents.) Read chapter 4, "Understanding Your Grief," on the process of grief to comprehend better the emotions that your friend may experience. The more you know about grief, the better able you will be to reach out to comfort your friend. You will feel less overwhelmed. If you have had a death in your family, you will know some of what your friend is going through right now. However, all grief is personal, and you can't fully know how another person feels when grief strikes.
- If you have had a death in your family, spend a few minutes remembering what was *not* helpful. Learn from your experience and gain insight into what not to say or do.
- Think about what *was* helpful and offer some of the same to your friend.
- Most likely, your friend would want you at the funeral or memorial service. However, if this is more than you can handle, perhaps you could do something else instead, such as house sitting while the family attends or helping prepare for a reception after the funeral. I recall the comment of a mother whose child

survived the Columbine, Colorado, school shooting: "My son cannot bring himself to attend the memorial," she said, "it is too much for him." If that is how you feel, it's OK. You be the judge.

- To help yourself further, ask your friend what will be happening. Will there be a viewing? What will happen at the funeral? Will there be another ceremony at the cemetery? If your friend is Jewish, will the family sit shiva? It is always good to know what rituals or customs may be taking place; you won't feel so awkward.

100. SHOULD YOU TALK ABOUT WHAT HAPPENED?

If you don't know whether you should talk about what happened, ask your friend. Say something like, "Would you like to talk about your brother? If you would, I'm here to listen. I'd like to know more." If your friend doesn't want to talk about it, you might suggest going out for a Coke and discussing other things. This gives your friend the right to choose. It gives him or her a little bit of control at a time when everything else seems out of control.

At the same time, be on the alert for your friend's feelings to change. It could happen that ten minutes later she decides to unload the whole story. Don't push the agenda; let her decide what to talk about and when. It is even OK to say, "You need to guide me as to what I can do that will be helpful."

101. PRACTICAL HELP YOU CAN PROVIDE

There are surely a lot of practical things that you can do, as people who are grieving need a lot of help getting organized and attending to details. Your friend may need help in getting homework assignments, updates on projects due, test dates, and the like. You could even offer to help him by doing your assignments together. A teen I met recently, whose father had died, told me that she was having a "Help Me Catch Up on Schoolwork" party over the weekend. Several friends were coming over for pizza and to help her focus on neglected homework.

102. WHAT DO YOU TELL OTHER PEOPLE?

If you are not sure of what information to pass on or to whom you pass it, ask your friend. Give him or her control over what you say. Depending on the circumstances of the death, there might be some details that are not for the general public to know. A teen whose father died discovered, after the death, some big financial problems her dad had. This became an embarrassment to her and her family. Other than sharing this with a friend, no one else needed to know these details.

103. RELAYING WORD TO THE SCHOOL

A teen, whose parents were divorced, got a phone call late one night to inform him that his mother had died in another state. He left immediately to be with family and to attend the funeral, leading to speculation by concerned friends and teachers on why he wasn't in school. It is for your friend to decide, of course, but in a case like this, you might offer to be an official messenger, informing the school and classmates on what happened. However, once again, let your friend decide, and be sure that you provide only the information he or she wants relayed. Watch out for rumors.

104. KEEP AN EYE ON HOW YOUR FRIEND IS COPING

Grief takes a long while. There will be times when your friend is fine, almost like his old self, and then there will be times when a lot of pent-up feelings come out. This is normal for grief. You will want to be available to your friend, no matter what stage he is in.

If you ever get worried about a friend and how she is coping, don't hesitate to suggest professional help. Search out resources for her. See if there is a support group nearby or ask the school counselor to start one. Go to the library and find some books on the topic or see if there is a counselor that specializes in grief. Make the initial phone calls and write down the information before you give it to your friend. Offer to go with her. I often see teens who bring friends along. Sometimes, a friend will even come to my bereaved-teen support group. If you accompany your friend when seeking help of this kind, you will gain valuable experience that may help in other situations later in life. (See topic 65, "What Happens When You See a Counselor?")

105. WHAT CAN YOU DO IF IT WAS YOUR FRIEND WHO DIED?

If it was your friend who died, how can you honor his or her memory best? One thing you can do is visit your friend's family somewhat as you did when your friend was alive. You could be an important link to the life of their dead child. If this feels awkward the first time, arrive with a gift, such as a small bouquet of flowers, a pizza, or some pictures of their daughter. It is OK, too, to invite the parents to events that their child would have attended, such as graduation, an important soccer game, or school play. They may decline, but that's all right. They will appreciate your asking. I know many parents who attend such things and are grateful to be included. I also know parents who cannot bring themselves to attend such events for fear of turning happy events into sad ones. I even know one mom who left town the day of graduation because she could not bear to hear the horns honking and see trees festooned with the traditional toilet paper in celebration.

106. SECRETS TOO BIG TO HANDLE

If your friend starts talking about something too big to handle, never hesitate to share this information with an adult. Big stuff, like wanting to die or big feelings of guilt, are too overwhelming for you to deal with. Get some help or advice, with your friend's permission if possible, but without it if necessary. You do not want to sit by and allow your friend to hurt herself—that's something you would regret for the rest of your life.

107. DON'T GET INTO A SORROW COMPETITION

This sometimes happens when a teenager dies, for instance in an auto accident. A competition will develop between his surviving friends, each wanting the world to know that she is hurting the most. I have worked with several teens who have gotten caught up in this kind of useless competition. In each case, they had a friend in common who had died, and suddenly various teens were competing for the distinction of having had the closest relationship with him. For example, one teen told me that she was getting a lot of support from friends after her boyfriend died, but was upset that another girl, who had dated the same guy years before, was doing a lot of crying and talking about the special relationship *she* had had with him. This sort of thing creates a lot of pain, and what is there to gain? If someone you were romantically involved with has died, try to see how pointless this kind of competition is. Mourn your loss, but don't advertise it. On the other hand, if you have a friend who seems to be slipping into such a competition, do all you can to convince her that the title "Girlfriend No. 1" is an empty honor hardly worthy of posting on the refrigerator door.

108. ARE YOU WORRIED ABOUT SAYING SOMETHING STUPID?

Are you worried that you might say something inappropriate or stupid? If you do, don't be too hard on yourself; we learn from our blunders. There are times that our anxiety over something will cause us to giggle at the wrong time or say something that comes out rather silly. Your friend will probably understand that you did not mean to make things worse. But here are some things to avoid saying:

• "I know how you feel." Even if you have had a death in your family, your grief is probably different. (See chapter 3, "Funerals, Formalities, and Farewells.") I have been in this work for many years, but if you have had a loved one die, I cannot say to you, "I know how you feel." I have a good idea of how you might be feeling, but I could be wrong. I really need for you to tell me.

• "You shouldn't feel that way." This comment often follows after a person has said that he feels guilty or responsible for something about the death. Even though what he is talking about makes no sense to you, it is important that you hear him out. The important fact is that he feels the guilt and is looking for someone to just listen. You don't have to fix it; he simply needs for you to be there. The comment "You shouldn't feel that way" gives a negative message to your friend, who is likely to tell himself, "I can't talk about this to this person." So where does this feeling go? If you are his closest friend, the likelihood is that it will go underground and cause big problems later. The real value in having a close friend is being able to say anything and know that you will be heard. (See topic 55, "Guilt and Regrets.")

• "It's part of God's plan." A faith in God and the life hereafter can be helpful, but when people tell me about this comment, they often feel angry and say, "Plan, what plan? Nobody asked me about any plan."

• "He's in a better place now." This may be true to your way of thinking, but your friend may not agree. (Who do you know who, given a choice, would choose that "better place" today?) She may think that her loved one was in a better place when he was alive and sharing her life here on earth.

• "Call me if you need anything." This is a limp statement. The bereaved often don't have the energy to call, and, anyway, they don't take statements like this seriously. But suppose that your friend did call for something just as you were going out on a date. Now what do you do? Instead of such vague offers, it would be more helpful if you had something specific you could offer, such as saying, "I have two hours free this afternoon. Could I help you with your homework or help in getting your room straightened out?"

• "Put it behind you now and get on with your life." This is easier said than done. The bereaved often wish that they could do just that, but statements like this make it sound like there's nothing to it. They are not appreciated.

109. OTHER THINGS TO AVOID

There are other things to avoid when reaching out to help your friend. Some might include the following:

• Don't do all the talking. Sometimes our anxiety causes us to rattle on, but silence really is golden. Your friend will appreciate your just being there. Or he will do all the talking and need someone just to listen.

- Avoid statements that begin with, "You should" or "You will." They are too directive and may not be what your friend really wants. For example, don't say "You should just forget what your family wants you to do" or "You shouldn't tell anyone how you are feeling" or "You will have to get angry with her for dying before you can work through your grief." We don't have the right to make those kinds of decisions and statements because we don't really know what is best.

- Don't discourage expressions of grief by changing the subject or leaving the room. If your friend starts to cry, hand her a tissue or give her a hug. If your friend needs to hit something, suggest you guys go out and shoot a few baskets. If your friend talks about guilt feelings, hear him out. If you don't know what to do to help, ask her.

- Don't promote your own values and beliefs. It may be very helpful to you to believe that Heaven exists, but your friend may not be so sure and might be offended if you push it. Or maybe your belief is that when someone takes their own life, they go to Hell. That could be very painful for your friend to hear. There are times to keep your values and beliefs to yourself. Your friend will ask you if he wants your input.

- Don't spread rumors or reveal private details. Some things are privileged information known only to you and your friend. Your friend needs to trust you. If you get pressured by others, tell them that you do not have permission to divulge that information. If they are so curious, they can ask the bereaved friend at a later time.

110. SOME GOOD THINGS TO SAY AND DO

We have been examining things *not* to say or do. Now let's look at some things that you *can* say or do that *will* be helpful and bring comfort and hope to your friend.

- Say "I'm sorry." This simple two-word statement says so much. Not only can you say this to your friend, but you can say it to your friend's family as well. Their response may also be a simple "Thank you." What do you say next? How about, "I am here to help. Can I run the vacuum? Run some errands? Pick people up at the airport?" Think of specific things you know might be helpful. However, if there is nothing for you to do, you might suggest that you and your friend go for a short walk. This would give him or her a chance to talk about what has happened and perhaps get some release from the intense atmosphere almost certainly prevailing at home.

- Send your friend a short letter of condolence. Even if you have been to the house and talked with everyone, it is still good manners to send a sympathy card with a short note. There are many fine cards on the market that address special losses, but you still need to write a sentence or two before signing your name. This condolence note needs to be written within a few days. If you wait too long, it gets harder to write. Over the years, I have learned how important these cards and notes are. Often people save them to reread for years to come. The notes that are most treasured are the ones that talk about the person who died, perhaps recounting stories previously unknown to the survivors, giving them new insights into the life and personality of that person. Sharing your memories of the person who died will reassure the bereaved that their loved one will not be forgotten. Or you might just write something like this:

  - "Your husband helped me a lot when I was getting started in Little League, and I will always be grateful that I had him as a manager."
  - "I want you to know that your wife was like a sister to me. She taught me sewing and helped me make my first dress. I will miss her terribly."

- "I have such wonderful memories of your son. Our long telephone talks, that vacation you invited me on, and his infectious laugh—I will remember Jack as long as I live."
- "I can't know how terrible this tragedy has been for you, but I do know that your daughter's death has been shattering to me. Please accept my heartfelt sympathy."

111. BEING A FRIEND CARRIES RESPONSIBILITIES

Being a friend carries certain responsibilities. As a friend, you can provide the kind of support that others can't so easily provide. Holding back at times of intense grief, thinking you don't want to impose yourself or, worse, being uncomfortable with grief may be the worst thing you could do. As a friend, you have a special role to play. You have something to offer that others can't—intimacy and confidentiality. You are even different from your friend's family, in that you have been chosen, invited, to be part of his or her life. Keep this thought in mind as you think about your friend and what you can do to help him or her through this painful experience.

Chapter 12

IS THAT ALL THERE IS?

Here we are, you and I, nearing the end of this painful excursion into a subject about which you never wanted to know in the first place. Your loved one is gone, and you may ask, "Is that all there is? You mean that I am expected to continue my life without this person who meant so much to me? Are you kidding?"

Is that how you feel? Well, I have known many teens who felt that way in the first few weeks or months after a loved one had died. Some of them have even said, "I won't accept it. I don't have to. It's not right."

You know, *accept* is an interesting word. Remember, we talked about it in chapter 5, "Understanding Your Feelings," when we were discussing denial. As you know, we accept gifts. We accept invitations. We accept compliments. But in all such cases, there is a choice. We don't have to accept gifts. We don't have to accept invitations. And we don't have to accept compliments from people who we think are insincere. But how can we *not* accept an earthquake, a flood, or the death of a loved one? We may not like it; we may hate it, but the event has occurred, and there is no undoing it.

If you are caught in that trap, let me suggest a way out of it. Intellectually, you know that your loved one is dead, but emotionally, you won't accept it. OK, don't accept it. Just tell yourself that the bad news arrived, all right, but you refused to sign for it. It's just sitting there, and you're not going to open it right now. You will open it when you get good and ready. But you know it's there. You aren't running away from it. You have a grip on reality.

There is nothing wrong with playing little games like this if they help you get through the difficult days that lie ahead. It's like telling yourself, "OK, I'm going to read just five more pages, and then I can go to bed," except that when that time comes, you give yourself another five-page assignment, and then another. It's the way we fool ourselves into accomplishing big things by doing many small things.

That's pretty much the way I expect you to begin rebuilding your life. You will do it in small steps. No huge leaps, no sweeping changes, but a few small steps here and there until one day you real-ize that life is worth living, after all.

It will be different, of course, from the life you would have had had your loved one not died. But in the end, each of us has a unique life to live. Even identical twins have their own separate lives to live. As much as you may feel that your life has been ruined, you still have your own inner self, your own character, your own set of talents, your own ideals, your own capacity to make something of your life, and, painful as it is to accept, the death of your loved one has not extin-guished that which is you.

Life will always be a mystery. How it began and how it evolved, we will never know. What accounts for genius? Who can explain a Michelangelo or a Shakespeare? How could Mozart have composed serious music at the age of five? What made Einstein such a brain? For that matter, how do you account for Elvis Presley or John Lennon and Paul McCartney? Life can be a disappointment, as it surely is to you right now, but you are still the same person with the same promise that you always had, and what you have to give the world is still there to be shaped and developed by you. You may yet turn out to be the greatest something-or-other in the history of the world!

Through your grief, you may also discover new things about your-self, qualities that you never knew you had. I know of a young father who went through a terrible ordeal when he thought that his baby daughter would die. He told me that the experience made him newly aware of other people's suffering, which he said he could somehow see in every face as he walked down the street. Like that man, you may come out of your grief a more complete, more rounded, more compassionate person.

In the lives of famous people you've read about in school, how many have been free of sadness and grief? In your study of history, how many historical figures have gone through life without personal tragedy? It's sobering, of course, to discover how unfair life can be, but it's reassuring, at the same time, to see that the human spirit can survive such cruelty.

Now, I know that nothing is more sobering than having tragedy strike you and that reading one book is not going to convince you that you can laugh again someday, that you will look forward to each new day with joy and expectation. Yet, I assure you that this will happen. When it does, you need not feel guilty, for every living thing is a survivor. The essence of life is rebirth. You see it in the rich, new growth after a great forest fire. You see it in the return of migratory birds every year. You see it in each new generation that populates the earth with its poets, thinkers, artists, and rascals of one kind or another. Hard as it may be for you to accept, life is a succession of losses—the loss of one's childhood, youth, dreams and fantasies, health, beauty, friends, and loved ones through the years—and yet our lives continue as we somehow come to accept and mourn each loss. The loss you have suffered is now a part of your life, just as the person who died lives on in your memory. Treasure that memory.

Resource List: Helpful Books and Web Sites

OTHER BOOKS ON TEEN GRIEF

Bode, Janet. *Death Is Hard to Live With: Teenagers Talk About How They Cope with Loss.* New York: Bantam Doubleday, 1993.

Grollman, Earl A. *Straight Talk About Death for Teenagers.* Boston: Beacon Press, 1993.

O'Toole, Donna. *Facing Change: Falling Apart and Coming Together Again in the Teen Years.* Burnsville, N.C.: Rainbow Publications, 1995.

WEB SITES ON GRIEF

http://www.beliefnet.com

In this site dedicated to the search for meaning in life, "The Grieving Teen" page appears in alternate months. Teens are encouraged to e-mail questions on issues of concern to them.

http://www.smartlink.net/~tag/index.html

Teen Age Grief, Inc., a nonprofit organization, has expertise in providing grief support to grieving teens.

http://www.aacap.org/factsFam/grief.htm

The American Academy of Child and Adolescent Psychiatry has helpful information on the grieving process.

http://www.hospicefoundation.org

The National Hospice Foundation provides links to hospices throughout the country.

http://www.dougy.org

The Dougy Center of Portland, Oregon, has helpful information on bereavement for people of all ages.

WEB SITES WITH INFORMATION ABOUT FUNERAL PRACTICES IN VARIOUS FAITHS

http://www.inthevillage.org/stjohns/funerals.htm

St. John's in the Village, a church in New York City, offers information about Episcopal Church funeral practices.

http://www.dsj.org/faq/cremation.htm

The Diocese of San Jose provides information about Catholic funeral practices, including cremation.

http://www.wct.org

The Woodlands, a Reform Jewish synagogue in White Plains, New York, provides information about Jewish funeral practices.

http://www.orst.edu/groups/msa/books/funeral.html

The Salman al-Farisi Islamic Center in Corvallis, Oregon, offers information on Islamic funeral practices.

http://www.isd.net/mboucher/choctaw/burial1.htm

Information on Choctaw funeral customs from the Choctaw Nation newspaper, *Bishinik*.

http://www.thinkquest.org/library/index.shtml

This library of in-depth educational materials created by students around the world covers subjects ranging from funeral practices to the Holocaust to black holes in space. It contains over two thousand sites.

http://www.aeu.org/loveis/index.html

The American Ethical Union offers a series of essays entitled "Love Is Stronger Than Death" by Arthur Dobrin.

INDEX

abandonment, 155, 165
abductions, 161, 162
absentmindedness, 80–82, 124, 176
academic performance, *see* schoolwork
accidents, 58, 59, 76, 82, 112, 130, 136, 138, 156
    automobile, 24, 44, 45–46, 50, 86, 101, 107, 111, 114, 134, 135, 148, 149–54, 164, 181–83, 186, 198
    gun, 152
    mountain-climbing, 44
    sailing, 44
    swimming, 148
addiction, 93
adolescents, *see* teenagers
affairs, extramarital, 155
AIDS, 156–57, 160
airplane crashes, 44, 50, 130, 150, 164
alcohol, 92, 93, 96, 105, 108, 125, 151, 153–54, 165, 181
American Academy of Child and Adolescent Psychiatry, 210
American Ethical Union, 211
American Red Cross, 160
anesthesia, 51–52, 148, 162
aneurysms, 44, 186
anger:
    coping with, 96–98, 121, 156
    in families, 95, 96, 98
    at God, 95, 180, 188–89, 200
    grief and, 74, 124, 126, 155
    illness and, 35, 179–81
    murder and, 161, 163
    physical symptoms of, 96–97
    self-directed, 98–100
    sources of, 94–96, 165
    suicide and, 109, 157, 158
    therapy for, 121
    validity of, 19, 35, 89, 94, 96
anniversaries, 140–42, 176, 184
anxiety:
    coping with, 123–27, 163, 174
    dreams caused by, 142–45
    of friends, 200
    illness and, 23, 110–11, 112
    trauma and, 40, 46, 147, 149, 164–67
apathy, 164
apologies, 36–37, 48, 101
apparitions, 145–46
arguments, 92
aromatherapy, 78
arrests, 84, 163
ashes, scattering of, 67, 68
aspirations, 18, 32, 85, 89, 92, 104, 107, 109–10, 113, 165, 169–70, 205–7
assassinations, 53, 86–87
automobile accidents, 24, 44, 45–46, 50, 86, 101, 107, 111, 114, 134, 135, 148, 149–54, 164, 181–83, 186, 198

Bach, Johann Sebastian, 127
back pain, 111, 124
bad news:
    details of, 49–50, 91, 159, 163, 196
    inaccuracy in, 49–50, 95, 138–39, 196

inappropriate responses to, 25–26, 95–96, 119–20, 176, 182, 199–200
in press reports, 45, 49–50, 57, 84, 95, 114, 138–39, 140
reaction to, 25–26, 205–6
relaying of, 33–34, 39, 45–46, 49–50, 83, 114–15, 196
rumors of, 49–50, 119, 196, 201
balloons, 48–49, 97, 101, 136, 151, 156
baths, 78
beliefs, personal, 200, 201
Bible, 33
birthdays, 140–42, 176
Bishinik, 211
bitterness, 19
blood pressure, 112
board games, 82
Bode, Janet, 209
bodies, 41–42, 43, 55, 57, 58, 59–60, 62, 148, 181, 182, 186, 195
body bags, 42
break time, 118
breath, shortness of, 165
breathing, deep, 78
burials, 57, 63–66, 195
burial services, 63–66, 195

call waiting, 29
cancer, 110, 156, 179–81, 187–91
carbon-monoxide poisoning, 148
cards, sympathy, 202–3
caskets, 48, 57, 58, 59–60, 65, 137, 159, 163, 182, 186, 195
Catholic Church, 210
celebrities, 53, 86–87, 139–40
cell phones, 82, 110
cemeteries, 64, 68–69, 102, 134, 195
change:
    acceptance of, 205–7
    coping with, 169–77
    sudden, 19, 109–10, 111
chaplains, hospital, 137
checklists, 80, 118
children, death of, 15, 24
chocolate, 77
Choctaw Nation, 211
Christmas, 141–42
churches, 59
city councils, 140
classes, resumption of, 115–19

clergy, 50, 64, 101, 108, 155, 167
closure:
    dreams and, 144–45
    good-byes as, 83, 84, 97, 136, 137, 163
coaches, 101, 108, 155
coffee, 77
coffins, *see* caskets
colds, 111, 112, 124
collages, 106
columbariums, 68
Columbine High School shootings, 17, 148, 195
comments, thoughtless, 95–96, 119–20, 176, 182, 199–200
community organizations, 94
community service, 153–54
compassion, 207
computers, 51, 110–11, 115, 145
concentration, problems with, 80–82, 116, 117, 125, 143, 165, 167
condolences, 59, 61, 134, 151, 153, 202–3
confessions, 102
confusion, 19, 23–24, 161
coroners, 41
corpses, 41–42, 43, 55, 57, 58, 59–60, 62, 148, 181, 182, 186, 195
counselors, school, 30, 46, 50, 51, 84, 94, 101, 105, 106, 108, 115, 121–23, 155, 167, 173, 180–81, 190–91
courtesy, 172
court system, 84
creativity, 63, 98, 106, 149, 158
cremation, 57, 63, 67–68, 159, 210
crematories, 67
crematoriums, 67
crying, 51–53, 65, 77, 82, 104, 136, 176, 180, 182, 185, 190, 198, 201
curfews, 99, 187, 188
Cynthia (case study), 184–87

dating, 104, 165, 170–74, 190, 200
daydreaming, 81
death, 39–53
    acceptance of, 205–7
    accidental, *see* accidents
    aftermath of, 113–27
    anniversary of, 140–42
    awareness of, 33–34, 85–86, 151

of children, 15, 24
comprehension of, 47
coping with, 39–53, 92, 93–94
denial of, 91–94, 102–3, 185, 186, 205
details of, 49–50, 91, 159, 163, 196
expected, 37–38, 74–75, 83, 85, 90
experience of, 40–41, 48, 66, 86, 135, 161–62, 163
fear of, 42–43, 109–11
finality of, 36, 63, 65–66, 69, 89–91
of friends, 86, 132–33, 135–36, 197–99
future plans altered by, 18, 32, 85, 89, 92, 104, 107, 109–10, 113, 165, 169–70, 205–7
multiple, 135–36, 157–58
near-, 43
notification of, 33–34, 39, 45–46, 49–50, 83, 114–15, 196
of parents, 19, 20, 25, 76, 85, 91, 92, 95, 99–100, 113, 119, 130, 169–74, 179–81, 183–84, 187–91
premonitions of, 183, 185
preoccupation with, 106–9, 122–23, 164
of public figures, 53, 86–87, 139–40
responsibility for, 151–54
secrets discovered after, 154–56
as separation, 36
shock of, 39–40, 43–46, 51–52, 83–84, 89–91, 124, 147–67, 184
of siblings, 76, 85–86, 181–87
sudden, 37, 44–45, 52, 74–75, 78, 83–84, 90, 91, 111, 136, 142, 164
timing of, 133–34
violent, 17, 45, 50, 74–75, 78, 83–84, 90, 91, 142, 147–67
wish for, 105, 106–9, 122–23, 150, 198
witnesses of, 147–49, 161
death certificates, 41
Death Is Hard to Live With (Bode), 209
"death rattle," 148
death wish, 105, 106–9, 122–23, 150, 198
debriefings, 149
decision making, 123, 125, 169, 201

denial:
of emotions, 73–74, 102–3, 164, 199–200
of reality, 91–94, 102–3, 185, 186, 205
of suicide, 156–57, 186
depressants, 93, 105
depression, 93, 96, 103–6
chronic, 184–85
clinical, 103, 105, 108
coping with, 105–6
medication for, 103
sources of, 103, 150, 164
symptoms of, 104–5, 120, 189–91
Diana, Princess, 86–87, 139
diaries, 51
digestion, 79, 112
diligence, 19
Diocese of San Jose, 210
disassociation, 47
disbelief, 89–91
disloyalty, 173
disobedience, 99
disrespect, 130
divorce, 15, 73, 196
Dixieland jazz funerals, 64
Dobrin, Arthur, 211
doctors, 40, 41, 83, 95, 112, 121, 188
doom, sense of, 46
Dougy Center, The, 210
"dream catchers," 145
dreams:
anxiety, 142–45
bad, 46, 50–51, 78, 84, 142–45, 162, 164
closure and, 144–45
day-, 81
good, 142, 143
journal on, 144
recurring, 46, 142–45
subconscious origin of, 50–51, 78, 143, 144, 146
talking about, 84, 144, 145
driving, 82, 153–54, 176
drugs, 92, 93, 96, 105, 108, 125, 151, 155, 160, 165, 181
drunk driving, 153–54

eating problems, 46, 78–79, 104, 127, 177, 190
Einstein, Albert, 117, 206

e-mail, 115
embalming, 43
embarrassment, 98, 105, 113, 116,
    119–20, 133, 139–40, 173, 180,
    181, 196
emergency services, 122
emotions, 89–112
    catalyst for, 52
    conflicting, 89
    coping with, 89–112, 123
    deadening of, 51–52, 89–91, 92, 93,
        148, 151, 162, 165
    denial of, 73–74, 102–3, 164,
        199–200
    expression of, 51–53, 90–91, 96,
        135, 153, 195
    internalized, 46, 52, 53, 73–74, 85,
        96, 199–200
    lack of, 85, 104
    negative, 92
    sharing of, 29–30, 46, 134
    understanding of, 89–112
    see also specific emotions
environmental tapes, 77–78, 127
Episcopal Church, 210
exercise, 78, 98, 104, 127, 153, 166, 177
extracurricular activities, 81

Facing Change (O'Toole), 209
failure, success vs., 127
families:
    anger in, 95, 96, 98
    conflicts in, 18, 92, 99, 124, 134,
        160, 170–74, 187
    extended, 30
    illness as viewed by, 23–25
    meetings of, 28
    murder and, 161, 162, 163
    relationships in, 85–86, 92, 95, 98
    secrets in, 154–56, 160
    suicide and, 157–58
    therapy for, 84, 166
    trauma and, 166–67
    withdrawal from, 15–16, 18, 92, 104
    see also parents; teenagers
fantasy, 93
farewells, see good-byes
fatalism, 117
fatigue, 33, 111, 112, 124, 165
fear:
    of abandonment, 155, 165

of death, 42–43, 109–11
of illness, 31–32
for personal safety, 46, 84, 111, 144,
    161
feelings, see emotions
finality, 36, 41, 47–48, 63, 65–66, 69,
    89–91, 188
financial problems, 32, 69, 113, 130, 196
fires, 152
flashbacks, 46, 84, 131–32, 164
flowers, 60, 137, 174, 197
flu symptoms, 111, 124
food, 46, 78–79
forgetfulness, 80–82, 124, 176
forgiveness, 102–3, 134, 152, 159
formalities, 48, 55–69
friends:
    anxiety of, 200
    curiosity of, 49–50, 84, 95
    death of, 86, 132–33, 135–36,
        197–99
    as funerals, 57–61, 64, 65, 90, 186,
        194–95, 196
    illness and, 26, 29, 99
    importance of, 15, 113
    keepsakes for, 132–33
    notification of, 114–15, 196
    respect of, 98
    responsibilities of, 203
    support of, 105, 115, 119–20, 122,
        123, 141, 159, 181, 182, 184,
        186–87, 193–203
    trust in, 26, 199–201, 203
funeral directors, 41, 57, 67
funeral homes, 41, 59, 68, 181
funerals, 48, 53, 55–69
    arrangements for, 57–58, 83, 107
    friends and relatives at, 57–61, 64,
        65, 90, 186, 194–95, 196
    good-byes at, 55–60, 84, 159
    Jewish, 61–62, 65, 195, 210–11
    laughter at, 61, 65, 66
    participation in, 56–59, 83, 90, 92,
        103, 135, 136–38, 153
    processions at, 64
    purpose of, 55
    "quickie," 158
    receptions after, 65–66, 194–95
    recording of, 58
    rituals of, 55, 56, 61–62, 65, 195,
        210–11

for suicides, 158–59
viewing of body in, 57, 58, 59–60, 182, 186, 195
future:
    plans for, 18, 32, 85, 89, 92, 104, 107, 109–20, 113, 165, 169–70, 205–7
    uncertainty of, 20

games, 33, 38, 82
gifts, 36, 120, 197
God, anger at, 95, 180, 188–89, 200
good-byes:
    as closure, 83, 84, 97, 136, 137, 163
    as final acts, 41, 47–48, 188
    at funerals, 55–69, 84, 159
    illness and, 24, 35–37, 180–81, 188
    importance of, 47–49, 75, 83
graduation, 197–98
grandparents, 85, 94
grave sites, 57, 63–69, 92, 102, 134, 136, 151, 156, 159
grief:
    anger and, 74, 124, 126, 155
    author as counselor on, 16, 121, 122, 123
    author's experiences of, 19, 25, 27, 28–29, 32, 49, 53, 59–60, 64, 73, 94, 95–96, 132, 137, 143, 170–71, 172, 174
    case histories of, 17, 20, 66, 179–91
    closure to, see closure
    community programs for, 16, 20, 94
    definition of, 71–72
    distraction by, 80–82, 116, 117, 124, 125, 143, 165, 167, 176
    emotional reactions to, 89–112
    intensity of, 71–74, 75, 83–84, 87, 103, 112, 120, 130, 175–77, 197, 203
    internalization of, 46, 52, 53, 73–74, 85, 96, 199–200
    isolation and, 15–16, 18, 47, 92, 104, 125, 159, 164, 167, 180, 186–87, 189
    literature on, 16, 17, 110–11, 145, 159, 160, 197, 209–10
    as normal, 71, 72–75, 116
    parental, 15, 66–67, 74
    patience and, 96, 120, 127
    physical symptoms of, 111–12

postponement of, 75, 129–30
problems from, 75–82
recovery from, 83, 167, 175–77, 191, 197, 205–7
relationships and, 85–87, 190
reminders and, 92, 131–33, 145–46
self-identity and, 75–77, 169–70, 197, 206–7
sharing of, 29–30, 55, 56, 59, 72, 93–94, 181
suicide and, 50, 86, 105, 106–9, 122–23, 132–33, 147, 150, 156–59, 164, 198, 201
support groups for, 30–31, 32, 94, 106, 107, 122, 159, 163, 197, 209–10
therapy for, 29–30, 46, 51, 84, 101, 103, 106, 121–23, 149, 153, 156, 159, 163, 166, 167, 197
understanding of, 71–87
unresolved, 93–94
Grollman, Earl A., 15–16, 209
group therapy, 166
guilt:
    coping with, 74, 100–103, 121, 134, 198, 199, 201
    emotional withdrawal and, 85, 199–200
    illness and, 180–81, 187–88
    learning from, 102
    perspective on, 154
    regret vs., 98–103, 152–53
    relief from, 100–103
    social life and, 29, 99–100
    sources of, 41, 48, 66, 86, 99–100, 135, 163
    suicide and, 157
    survivor, 149–51, 165, 207
gun accidents, 152

hallucinations, 145–46, 164
happiness, 19, 109, 165, 175, 185, 207
headaches, 111, 124
headstones, 68–69
healing:
    memorial services and, 62–63
    time for, 83, 167, 175–77, 191, 197, 205–7
health, 94–95, 111–12, 124, 127, 166
health workers, 40, 41
heart attacks, 44, 147–48, 156, 188

heartbeat, rapid, 165
heart problems, 44, 112, 147–48, 156, 188
Heath High School shootings, 17
help, practical, 195–96, 202
hindsight, 100–101
holidays, 140–42, 176, 184
homework, 33, 80, 81, 104, 106, 113, 114, 117–19, 177, 196
  see also schoolwork
homosexuality, 160
hospices, 30–31, 40, 41, 94, 210
hospitals:
  deaths in, 41
  visits to, 33–34, 99, 179–81
housecleaning, 19
house sitting, 194–95
hugs, 60, 119, 120, 136, 167, 201
humor, sense of, 126
hygiene, personal, 104

idealization, 76–77, 164, 183
illness:
  anger and, 35, 179–81
  anxiety and, 23, 110–11, 112
  behavior affected by, 28–29
  causes of, 94–95, 99
  confusion about, 23–24
  counseling and, 29–30
  critical, 130
  disfiguring, 59, 180
  family's response to, 23–25
  fatigue and, 33
  fear of, 31–32
  friends and, 26, 29, 99
  good-byes and, 24, 35–37, 180–81, 188
  guilt and, 180–81, 187–88
  information on, 110–11, 160
  new responsibilities and, 27–28, 188
  outside support and, 26–27, 30–31
  pain in, 24, 42, 189
  prolonged, 37–38, 179–81
  shock of, 23–24, 124, 188–91
  social life and, 28–29
  sudden, 37
  support groups for, 30–31
  teachers and, 26–27
  terminal, 15, 23–38
  truth of, 24–25
immune system, 111

information:
  importance of, 24, 34–35, 42
  inaccurate, 49–50, 95, 138–39, 196
  incomplete, 19, 91
  retaining of, 117
  sources of, 16, 17, 110–11, 145, 159, 160, 197, 209–11
insomnia, 35, 43, 77–78, 104, 111, 123, 124, 127, 165, 177, 190
intellectualizing, 89–91, 97
internalization, 46, 52, 53, 73–74, 85, 96, 199–200
Internet, 110–11, 145, 209–11
Islam, 210
isolation, 15–16, 18, 47, 92, 104, 125, 164, 167, 180, 186–87, 189

Jews, 61–62, 65, 195, 210
jobs, 93
Johns Hopkins University, 110–11
journals, personal, 97, 102, 132, 134, 144, 146
justice, 161, 163

Karen (case study), 187–91
keepsakes, 106, 132–33
Kennedy, John F., 53, 86–87, 139
Kennedy, Robert F., 86–87
King, Martin Luther, Jr., 86–87
Koran, 33

laughter, 61, 65, 66, 126
laundry, 27, 28
Laura (case study), 17
lawyers, 153
letters, 48, 52, 97, 102, 134, 136, 137, 139, 149, 151, 156, 163, 202
lies, 99, 155, 186
life:
  celebration of, 60, 63
  getting on with, 113–27, 175–77, 205–7
  meaning of, 19, 150
  unfairness of, 19, 35, 207
Life After Life (Moody), 43
"life problems," 121
listening, 199–201
loneliness, 15–16, 125, 186–87
love:
  evidence of, 156, 157

expressions of, 35, 36, 48, 49
  unconditional, 87
"Love Is Stronger Than Death"
  (Dobrin), 211

mausoleums, 68
Mayo Clinic, 110
meals, 19, 28, 29, 78–79
medication, 103, 166
meditation, 77, 127, 166
Megan (case study), 179–81
mementos, 106, 132–33
memorabilia, 106, 132–33
memorials, 138, 140, 195
memorial services, 59, 62–63, 67, 83,
  84, 86, 137, 140
memories:
  blank spots in, 164
  enjoyment of, 73, 156, 160, 176, 207
  problems with, 80, 117, 164
  sharing of, 36–37, 57, 61, 65, 93,
    105, 131, 142, 149, 202–3
  traumatic, 46, 84, 131–32, 148–49,
    164
mental-health centers, 16, 30–31, 94,
  106, 108, 121–22, 167
Mental Health Services (Fairfax
  County, Va.), 16
mental illness, 121, 122–23
mental tricks, 145–46
military casualties, 45, 92
Monroe, Marilyn, 139
Moody, Raymond A., Jr., 43
morgues, 41
mortality, awareness of, 33–34, 85–86,
  151
mountain-climbing accidents, 44
mourning, 72–73, 103, 114, 160, 176,
  198–99, 207
movies, 78
murder, 50, 84, 144, 152, 161–63, 164
music, 38, 57, 78, 97, 102, 104, 118,
  127, 131, 145, 146, 165, 166,
  176, 206

Natalie (case study), 183–84
National Hospice Foundation, 210
Native Americans, 145, 211
nausea, 111, 182
near-death experiences, 43
news, bad, see bad news

newspapers, 45, 49–50, 57, 84, 95, 114,
  138–39, 140
night-lights, 145, 146
nightmares, 46, 50–51, 78, 84, 142–45,
  162, 164
noise, 165
notebooks, 51, 117
notes, suicide, 157, 185–86
notes, sympathy, 202–3
numbness, 51–52, 89–91, 92, 93, 148,
  151, 162, 165

objectivity, 120, 154
organ donations, 83
orphans, 76
O'Toole, Donna, 209
overwhelmed, feeling, 104, 105, 109,
  125, 165

pain:
  avoidance of, 91–92, 164, 165
  blocking of, 51–52, 89–91, 92, 93,
    148, 151, 162, 165
  emotional, 51–53, 56, 58, 73, 83, 89,
    90–93, 102, 107, 109, 114, 129,
    148, 155–56
  physical, 24, 42, 51–52, 111, 124,
    148, 189
  sharing of, 51–53, 56, 58, 90–93,
    155–56
  temporary, 109
panic attacks, 46, 110
parents:
  counselors and, 123
  dating by, 170–74
  death of, 19, 20, 25, 76, 85, 91, 92,
    95, 99–100, 113, 119, 130,
    169–74, 179–81, 183–84,
    187–91
  events attended by, 197–98
  grand-, 85, 94
  grief of, 15, 66–67, 74
  single, 76
  step-, 174
  support of, 76, 106, 108, 116, 123,
    170–74
  teenagers vs., 18, 92, 99, 124, 134,
    160, 170–74, 187, 188
  working, 19
parties, 29
patience, 96, 120, 127

peer groups, 95, 124
penance, 102
perfectionism, 127
Persian Gulf War, 45
perspective, 120, 154
pets, death of, 87, 94
phone calls, 29, 32, 35, 82, 104, 110, 118, 173, 197, 200
photographs, 57, 59, 60, 73, 93, 132, 137, 142, 197
Phyllis (case study), 66
poetry, 52, 69, 102, 106, 137
police, 163
Pope, Alexander, 103
pornography, 155
positive thinking, 126
post-traumatic stress disorder (PTSD), 40, 46, 147, 149, 164–67
    coping with, 165–67
    symptoms of, 164–65
prayer, 41, 137
prayer service, 137
premonitions, 183, 185
Presley, Elvis, 139, 206
press reports, 45, 49–50, 57, 84, 95, 114, 138–39, 140
prioritization, 109, 118
problem solving, 125, 126–27
processions, funeral, 64
procrastination, 126
psychiatrists, 121, 166
psychologists, 29–30, 121
public figures, 53, 86–87, 139–40
public service, 140, 151, 153–54

questions, asking of, 34–35, 42, 50, 113–14, 135, 138, 158, 159

rage, 155
rape, 162
rationalizations, 125
reading, 78, 117, 177
reality:
    denial of, 91–94, 102–3, 185, 186, 205
    disbelief in, 89–91
regrets, 37, 56, 98–103, 134, 152–53
rejection, 155
relationships, 93, 165
    in families, 85–86, 92, 95, 98
    grief and, 85–87, 190

relatives, 57–61, 64, 65, 90, 186, 194–95, 196
relaxation, 77–78, 126, 127, 166
relief, feelings of, 51, 65, 100–103, 153
religion, 59, 61–62, 64–65, 195, 200, 201, 210–11
remarriage, 170–74
reminders, 92, 131–33, 145–46
resentment, 134
resource list, 209–10
responsibilities, personal, 15, 19, 27–28, 95, 117–18, 123, 169–70, 188, 189, 203
revenge, 161
rewards, 118
rigor mortis, 43
rituals, 55, 56, 61–62, 65, 176, 195, 210
rivalry, 18, 198–99
rock climbing, 138
role models, 182–83
Romeo and Juliet (Shakespeare), 158
routines, 81–82, 106, 110, 113, 116–19, 166, 167, 169, 177
rumors, 49–50, 119, 196, 201

sadness, 49, 55, 125, 133, 139–40, 189, 190–91, 207
safety, personal, 46, 84, 111, 144, 161
sailing accidents, 44
St. John's in the Village, 210
Salman al-Farisi Islamic Center, 210
SATs, 129
schedules, 81–82, 105, 110, 113, 116–19, 166, 167, 169, 177
schoolwork, 46, 75, 77, 81–82, 92, 93, 99, 115–19, 123, 124, 125, 129, 143, 154, 164, 189–90
    see also homework
Scott (case study), 181–83
scrapbooks, 106
second-guessing, 100–101
secrets, 154–56, 160, 198, 201
sedatives, natural, 77
self-destructiveness, 96, 100, 108, 157–58, 165
self-esteem, 98, 100–101, 104, 134, 177
self-identity, 65, 75–77, 169–70, 197, 206–7
sex, 105, 125, 160, 181
Shakespeare, William, 158, 206

shame, 18, 98, 105
shootings, school, 17, 46, 148, 195
shopping, 27
showers, 78
siblings:
  care of, 27, 34
  death of, 76, 85–86, 181–87
  rivalry of, 18
silence, moment of, 140
"Silent Night," 57
sitting shiva, 56, 61–62, 195
sleeping, 35, 43, 77–78, 104, 111, 112,
  123, 124, 127, 165, 177, 190
smoking, 94, 99
social life, 28–29, 99–100, 104
sorrow:
  competition in, 198–99
  expressions of, 59, 61, 134, 151,
    153, 202–3
sound machines, 127
spirit, 65
stepparents, 174
stigma, 18, 75–76, 113
stimulants, 77, 93
stomach upset, 124
stories, 61, 65, 105, 142, 167, 202–3
Straight Talk About Death for Teenagers
  (Grollman), 16, 209
stress, 123–27
  levels of, 121
  management of, 123–27, 174
  negative, 124
  relief from, 51, 153
  sources of, 123–24
  symptoms of, 111–12, 124–25
  talking about, 125–26
  trauma and, 39–40, 46, 147, 149,
    164–67
strokes, 188
study hall, 117
study routines, 81–82, 116–19
subconscious, 50–51, 78, 143, 144, 146
suicide, 156–59
  anger and, 109, 157, 158
  coping with, 150, 152, 156–59
  denial of, 156–57, 186
  families and, 157–58
  funerals for, 158–59
  grief and, 50, 86, 105, 106–9,
    122–23, 132–33, 147, 150,
    156–59, 164, 198, 201

  guilt and, 157
  multiple, 157–58
  survivors of, 150, 156–59, 183–87
superhuman qualities, 76–77, 164, 183
support groups, 30–31, 32, 94, 106,
  107, 122, 159, 163, 197, 209–10
survivors, 149–51, 156–59, 165,
  183–87, 207
swimming accidents, 148
sympathy, 59, 61, 134, 151, 153, 202–3

tape recorders, 98, 137
tasks, self-assigned, 102
tea, 77
teachers:
  illness and, 26–27
  memorial services for, 62–63
  notification of, 114, 115, 196
  shooting of, 46
  support of, 26–27, 46, 81–82, 95,
    114–19
Teen Age Grief, Inc., 209
teenagers:
  case studies of, 179–91
  as category, 17–18
  as emerging adults, 17–19, 182–83
  grieving, *see* grief
  inner world of, 15
  parents vs., 18, 92, 99, 124, 134,
    160, 170–74, 187, 188
  peer groups of, 95, 124
  responsibilities of, 15, 19, 27–28, 95,
    117–18, 123, 169–70, 188, 189,
    203
  social life of, 28–29, 99–100, 104
  support groups for, 30–31, 32, 94,
    106, 107, 122, 159, 163, 197,
    209–10
television, 33, 38, 45, 49, 81, 138–39,
  140, 177
temper, loss of, 124, 126
tenseness, 96–97
therapy, 29–30, 46, 51, 84, 101, 103,
  106, 121–23, 149, 153, 156, 163,
  166, 167, 197
thoughts, control of, 100
Thurston High School shootings, 17
trauma:
  anxiety and, 40, 46, 147, 149,
    164–67
  families and, 166–67

memory and, 46, 84, 131–32,
148–49, 164
as shock, 39–40, 43–46, 51–52,
83–84, 89–91, 124, 147–67, 184
stress and, 39–40, 46, 147, 149,
164–67
see also post-traumatic stress
disorder
trials, murder, 163
trust, 26, 155, 199–201, 203
tumors, brain, 28–29
"tunnel vision," 127
twins, identical, 206

"unfinished" business, 36, 47–48, 83,
84, 133, 136
urns, 67–68

very personal anniversaries (VPAs), 141
veterans, 122
victims, identities of, 49

videos, home, 106, 137
viewing of body, 57, 58, 59–60, 182,
186, 195
violent deaths, 17, 45, 46, 50, 74–75,
78, 83–84, 90, 91, 142, 147–67
vision, blurred, 82
voices, 145

wakes, 56
walks, 118, 120, 127, 166, 202
weekends, study, 118
weight problems, 79, 94, 104, 112
wishes, 99, 105, 106–9
wish lists, 132
witnesses, 147–49, 161
Woodlands, The, 210
work ethic, 19
World War II, 122
worries, 109–11, 161
writing, 47, 48, 51, 52, 97, 102, 117,
132, 134, 137, 144, 146